ORDINAL AND
SERVICE BOOK

ORDINAL AND SERVICE BOOK

FOR USE IN
COURTS OF THE CHURCH

THE CHURCH OF SCOTLAND

NEC TAMEN CONSUMEBATUR

PREPARED BY THE GENERAL ASSEMBLY'S
COMMITTEE ON PUBLIC WORSHIP
AND AIDS TO DEVOTION

GEOFFREY CUMBERLEGE
OXFORD UNIVERSITY PRESS
LONDON GLASGOW NEW YORK

Oxford University Press, Amen House, London E.C.4

GLASGOW NEW YORK TORONTO MELBOURNE WELLINGTON
BOMBAY CALCUTTA MADRAS KARACHI CAPE TOWN IBADAN

Geoffrey Cumberlege, Publisher to the University

FIRST PUBLISHED 1931
SECOND EDITION (O.U.P.) 1954

PRINTED IN GREAT BRITAIN

PREFACE

This Ordinal and Service Book was first issued in 1931, to give guidance to presbyteries in the re-united Church of Scotland. Having fallen out of print, it has now been slightly revised, as for example in the Service for Holy Communion, to bring this service into conformity in its principal parts to the Book of Common Order; and other services have been shortened, where possible. New matter has been added, as in the Service for the Consecration of a Hall-Church, and a new service for the Licensing of Probationers has been inserted. Emphasis, too, has been laid upon the appropriateness of sermons at services of ordination and induction being closely related to the action; and charges have been prepared which are the voice of the Church in the New Testament rather than of an individual minister. The Committee commends this book to the use of presbyteries and other courts of the Church, and trusts that it will meet a felt need.

WILLIAM D. MAXWELL, D.D.

Convener

NOTE

THE prayers and forms in this book are drawn from a number of sources, many of them classical but some modern and therefore copyright. Any application for permission to reproduce material from this book should be addressed in the first instance to the publishers.

CONTENTS

The Orders which follow are recommended by the Committee on Public Worship and Aids to Devotion for use in Church Courts.

On the day appointed for any of the Services which follow, the Presbytery shall meet beforehand in a place adjoining the church, and be constituted by the Moderator.

The chancel or sanctuary, and a sufficient number of adjacent pews in the church, shall be reserved for the Presbytery, and Bibles and hymnaries provided for them.

Robes shall be worn by the officiating Ministers and by all other Ministers of the Presbytery.

Probationers and Lay Readers at their licensing shall wear a gown.

An Ordinand at his ordination shall wear cassock and gown, but without bands.

A Minister at his induction shall wear his customary robes.

Members of the Presbytery shall enter the church in this order: the Elders first, then the Ordinand, the Minister to be inducted, or the Candidates for Licence, and thereafter the Ministers in order of their ordination, those that are junior leading, and seats being reserved for those that are senior nearest to the officiating Ministers, who enter last. All shall remain standing in their appointed places in the church, until the officiating Ministers have taken their seats.

Suitable provision shall be made for the Ordinand, the Minister who is to be inducted, or the Candidates for Licence to kneel. A table, other than the Communion Table, should be made ready for the signing of the Formula.

The portions of the following orders enclosed within brackets may be omitted.

1

FORM AND ORDER FOR THE LICENSING OF PROBATIONERS FOR THE HOLY MINISTRY*

The Licensing of Probationers shall take place in a church, in the presence of a congregation, preferably, when there is but one candidate, the congregation of which he is a member, and with the deliberation and dignity befitting so solemn an office.

The Moderator of Presbytery shall conduct the Service, but another Minister may be appointed to preach the sermon, or otherwise to assist, as may be convenient.

At the time appointed, the Presbytery being constituted and the congregation assembled, and the Candidates for Licence having taken their places before the Presbytery, the Service shall begin with the singing of Psalm lxxxiv. 1–2, 10–12, *to the tune* Harington, *concluding with the doxology.*

Thereafter the Moderator shall say:

OUR help is in the name of the Lord, who made heaven and earth.

How beautiful upon the mountains are the feet

---

* *This service may be used for the Licensing of Lay Readers; when so used the words 'Lay Reader' shall be substituted throughout for 'Probationer' or 'Probationer for the Holy Ministry'.*

of him that bringeth good tidings, that publisheth peace.

Let us pray.

ALMIGHTY God, without whom we can do no good thing; grant us now the aid of Thy divine grace, that the prayers which we offer and the vows which we take before Thee may be acceptable unto Thee; through Jesus Christ our Lord. AMEN.

℣. Lord have mercy upon us.

℟. Christ have mercy upon us.

℣. Lord have mercy upon us.

WE acknowledge, O God, that we are not worthy to approach unto Thee or to do anything in Thy Name. We have sinned grievously against Thee in thought, in word, and in deed. Mercifully forgive us, we beseech Thee, and absolve us from all our sins; for the sake of Jesus Christ, Thy Son, our Lord. AMEN.

O GOD, whose mercies are new every morning, fresh every moment, and more than we can number; we praise Thy holy Name that by the glad sound of the Gospel Thou dost call us to have part in Thy kingdom and glory. We bless Thee that Thou dost bestow heavenly gifts of power and utterance upon those whom Thou dost choose to be the stewards of Thy holy mysteries. Grant, we beseech Thee, a full measure of Thy Spirit to the Church in our time, that she may so declare the Gospel to the world that all men everywhere may be won to Thine obedience. Lord of the harvest, send forth labourers into Thine harvest. Endow Thy ministers with the Holy Spirit, and cause Thy Church to increase in righteousness, wisdom, and peace to the glory of Thy holy Name; through Jesus Christ our Lord, to whom with Thee and the Holy Spirit be glory and praise, world without end. AMEN.

Then shall the following Lessons from holy Scripture be read: Isaiah vi. 1–8; 2 Timothy i. 1–14.

Thereafter, the Apostles' Creed shall be said by all, standing:

I BELIEVE in God the Father Almighty, Maker of heaven and earth:

And in Jesus Christ His only Son our Lord, Who was conceived by the Holy Ghost, Born of the Virgin Mary, Suffered under Pontius Pilate, Was crucified, dead, and buried, He descended into hell; The third day He rose again from the dead, He ascended into heaven, And sitteth on the right hand of God the Father Almighty; From thence He shall come to judge the quick and the dead.

I believe in the Holy Ghost; The holy Catholic Church; The Communion of Saints; The Forgiveness of sins; The Resurrection of the body; And the life everlasting. AMEN.

Then shall be sung the hymn, Veni Creator Spiritus, Come, Holy Ghost, our souls inspire.

Thereafter, the Moderator shall declare as follows:

IN the Name of the Lord Jesus Christ, the King and Head of the Church, who, being ascended on high, hath given gifts unto men for the edifying of the body of Christ, we are met here as a Presbytery to license N. N. [and M. M.] as preacher[s] of the Gospel and probationer[s] for the holy Ministry.

In this act the Church of Scotland, as part of the

Holy Catholic or Universal Church worshipping one God, Father, Son, and Holy Spirit, affirms anew its belief in the Gospel of the sovereign grace and love of God, wherein through Jesus Christ, His only Son, our Lord, incarnate, crucified, and risen, He freely offers to all men, upon repentance and faith, the forgiveness of sins, renewal by the Holy Spirit, and eternal life, and calls them to labour in the fellowship of faith for the advancement of the kingdom of God throughout the world.

The Church of Scotland acknowledges the Word of God, which is contained in the Scriptures of the Old and New Testaments, to be the supreme rule of faith and life.

The Church of Scotland holds as its subordinate standard the Westminster Confession of Faith, recognizing liberty of opinion on such points of doctrine as do not enter into the substance of the Faith, and claiming the right, in dependence on the promised guidance of the Holy Spirit, to formulate, interpret, or modify its subordinate standards: always in agreement with the Word of God and the fundamental doctrines of the Christian Faith contained in the said Confession, of which agreement the Church itself shall be sole judge.

Then the Moderator, addressing the Candidate or Candidates, who are to stand and make answer to the questions put to them, shall say:

IN view of this Declaration you are now required to answer these questions:

DO you believe in one God, Father, Son, and Holy Spirit; and do you confess anew the Lord Jesus Christ as your Saviour and Lord?
    Answer. I do.

DO you believe the Word of God, which is contained in the Scriptures of the Old and New Testaments, to be the supreme rule of faith and life?

Answer. I do.

DO you believe the fundamental doctrines of the Christian Faith contained in the Confession of Faith of this Church?

Answer. I do.

DO you acknowledge the Presbyterian government of this Church to be agreeable to the Word of God; and do you promise to be subject in the Lord to this Presbytery, or any Presbytery within whose bounds you may reside, and to the superior courts of the Church?

Answer. I do.

DO you promise to seek the unity and peace of this Church; to uphold the doctrine, worship, government, and discipline thereof; and to cherish a spirit of brotherhood towards all the followers of the Lord?

Answer. I do.

ARE not zeal for the glory of God, love to the Lord Jesus Christ, and a desire for the salvation of men, so far as you know your own heart, your great motives and chief inducements to enter into the office of the holy Ministry?*

Answer. They are.

* *At the Licensing of Lay Readers, this vow and the words enclosed in brackets of the vow following shall be omitted.*

DO you engage in the strength of the Lord Jesus Christ to live a godly and circumspect life; [and faithfully, diligently, and cheerfully to discharge the duties of your ministry,] seeking in all things the advancement of the kingdom of God?

Answer. I do.

The questions having been answered to the satisfaction of the Presbytery, the Moderator shall call upon the Candidate or Candidates to sign the Formula, saying:

YOU are required now to sign the Formula, as a seal of these vows which you have made.

The signing being completed, the Candidate or Candidates shall kneel, and the Moderator shall say:

Let us pray.

DIRECT us by Thy Holy Spirit, we humbly beseech Thee, O Lord, and assist us with Thy grace as in the Name of Thy blessed Son we set apart these Thy servants to the preaching of the Gospel. Graciously accept them as they dedicate themselves to Thy service, and bestow on them the grace of the Holy Spirit. Give them such power of understanding and utterance that, as they preach the unsearchable riches of Christ, they may be enabled to enlighten the ignorant, guide the perplexed, and gather into Thy fold those that are gone astray. Let Thy word on their lips bring good tidings to the weary and heavy laden, and comfort to them that mourn.

[Spare them, if it please Thee, that in due time they may be called and ordained to the office of the holy Ministry. Grant them the assurance that Thy word cannot return unto Thee void, and give to Thy Church the abundant fruit of their labours.]*

Sanctify and confirm them in their work and witness by Thy heavenly benediction; that, holding fast their profession without wavering, they may finish their course with joy, and finally of Thy mercy receive a full reward in Thy heavenly kingdom; through Jesus Christ our Lord, who liveth and reigneth with Thee and the Holy Spirit, one God, world without end. AMEN.

AND now, as our Saviour Christ hath taught us, we pray, saying,

OUR Father . . .

Prayer being ended, the Moderator shall declare as follows:

IN the Name of the Lord Jesus Christ, and by the authority which He has given to His Church, we do now license and commission you to preach the Gospel of His grace wherever God in His providence shall call you.

Then the Moderator may deliver to each Probationer a copy of the Holy Scriptures, saying:

TAKE now this Bible, of which you are appointed an interpreter; and be diligent to study the things which are written therein; that, as much as in you lies, you may faithfully and truly teach the Gospel of the grace of God, and be an example of faith and holy living.

* *When this service is used for the Licensing of Lay Readers, this paragraph shall be omitted.*

Then he shall bless the Probationer or Probationers, saying:

THE blessing of the Father, and of the Son, and of the Holy Spirit, be with you, and rest upon you. The Lord be in your heart, and in your lips, that you may worthily declare His holy Gospel. AMEN.

The hymn Spirit of God, descend upon my heart, *or,* Christ is made the sure foundation, *shall now be sung.*

Thereafter the Moderator, or another appointed to do so, shall deliver a Charge to those who have been licensed.

The Charge being concluded, a celebration of Holy Communion may follow; or Psalm lxvii *shall be sung, with doxology, to the tune* Selma, *and the Service shall end with the Benediction:*

THE peace of God, which passeth all understanding, keep your hearts and minds in the knowledge and love of God, and of His Son Jesus Christ our Lord; and the blessing of God Almighty, the Father, the Son, and the Holy Ghost, be amongst you, and remain with you always. AMEN.

Before the meeting of Presbytery is closed, the Presbyters shall give the Probationer[s] the right hand of welcome.

2

FORM AND ORDER
FOR THE
ORDINATION OF MINISTERS

*The Presbytery having been constituted by the Modera-
tor, the Edict shall be produced, duly executed; the
prescribed intimation shall be made concerning objections, and, if none be offered, the Presbytery shall resolve to proceed with the Ordination.*

Divine Service shall begin with the singing of Psalm
lxv. 1–4, *to the tune* St. Stephen, *concluding with the
doxology.*

*Thereafter the Minister appointed to take the first part
of the Service shall say:*

OUR help is in the Name of the Lord, who made
heaven and earth.

One thing have I desired of the Lord, that will I
seek after; that I may dwell in the house of the Lord
all the days of my life, to behold the beauty of the
Lord, and to enquire in His temple.

Let us pray.

ALMIGHTY God, who hast made the Church
Thy dwelling place; be pleased to manifest Thyself to us Thy servants who meet this day in Thy
holy place; and inspire our hearts to worship Thee

in spirit and in truth; through Jesus Christ our Lord. AMEN.

O GOD, most holy and most merciful, we confess that we have sinned against Thee and against one another. We have been disobedient to Thy will, unthankful for Thy mercies, and unfaithful to the trust committed to our hands.

Have mercy upon us, O Lord, have mercy upon us; and graciously forgive all our iniquities. Cast us not away from Thy presence, and take not Thy Holy Spirit from us; but bestow on us Thy pardon and peace; through Jesus Christ our Lord. AMEN.

ALMIGHTY Father, accept us as we dedicate ourselves anew to Thee; and enable us by Thy grace to obey Thee in all things, and to yield our hearts and lives to Thy service. Grant unto us, we beseech Thee, a purer love towards Thee, a deeper devotion to our Lord and Saviour, a truer loyalty to Thy Church, and a stronger desire to further Thy kingdom and to glorify Thy Name; through Jesus Christ our Lord, who liveth and reigneth with Thee and the Holy Spirit, world without end. AMEN.

Then shall be read a Lesson from the Old Testament: Isaiah lxi. 1–6.

Psalm lxviii. 18–20 *shall now be sung, to the tune* Winchester, *concluding with the doxology.*

And these Lessons from the New Testament shall be read: 1 St. Peter v. 1–4; St. John xxi. 15–17.

Then the Apostles' Creed shall be said by all, standing:

I BELIEVE in God the Father Almighty, Maker of heaven and earth:

And in Jesus Christ His only Son our Lord, Who was conceived by the Holy Ghost, Born of the Virgin Mary, Suffered under Pontius Pilate, Was crucified, dead, and buried, He descended into hell; The third day He rose again from the dead, He ascended into heaven, And sitteth on the right hand of God the Father Almighty; From thence He shall come to judge the quick and the dead.

I believe in the Holy Ghost; The holy Catholic Church; The Communion of Saints; the Forgiveness of sins; The Resurrection of the body; And the life everlasting. AMEN.

Thereafter, the Minister shall say,

Let us pray.

O LORD our God, who hast founded Thy Church upon earth, and hast promised to abide with it for ever; enlighten and sanctify it, we beseech Thee, by Thy Holy Spirit.

We pray for all Ministers of Thy Word and Sacraments; that Thou wouldst increase in them Thy grace, that with joy and assurance they may guard and feed Thy sheep, looking to the great Shepherd and Bishop of souls.

We pray for this congregation and parish; that Thou wouldst encompass them with Thy favour, and grant that with one heart and one mind they may strive together for the faith of the Gospel.

We pray for the progress of Thy kingdom throughout all the world; that Thou wouldst hasten the time when in the Name of Jesus every knee shall bow, and every tongue confess that He is Lord.

We pray for kings and for all in authority, especially for our Sovereign Lady Queen Elizabeth and all her house; for the Queen's Ministers and Counsellors, and for the people of this realm; that Thou wouldst exalt our land in righteousness, and guide the nations in the way of peace.

We pray for the afflicted, for those who are lonely and sad, for those in sickness and sorrow, and for all whom we name in our hearts; that Thou wouldst lift up the fallen, strengthen the weak, and comfort them that mourn; through Jesus Christ our Lord. AMEN.

WE bless and praise Thy Name, O God, for Thy saints, martyrs, and confessors, for all Thy servants departed this life in Thy faith and fear, and for those dear to us who are now with Thee; and we beseech Thee that Thou wouldst keep us united to them in the communion of Thy saints, and finally gather us with them in the glory of Thy kingdom; through Jesus Christ our Lord, to whom, with Thee and the Holy Spirit, we ascribe glory and honour, thanksgiving and power, world without end. AMEN.

Then shall be sung the hymn, The Church's one foundation.

A Sermon shall be preached on the holy Ministry, and may contain counsel to both Minister and people; in which case the subsequent Charges shall be those printed on pages 19–20.

[*Where the Service is one for the induction of a Minister already ordained, the rest of the Service to be used is to be found at page 26.*]

Thereafter, the Narrative shall be read, and, the Ordinand having taken his place before the Presbytery, the Moderator shall say:

IN the name of the Lord Jesus Christ, the King and Head of the Church, who, being ascended on high, hath given gifts unto men for the edifying of the body of Christ, we are met here as a Presbytery to ordain N. N. to the Office of the holy Ministry by prayer and the laying on of hands by the Presbyters to whom it doth belong,* [and to induct him into the Pastoral Charge of M.]

In this act of ordination the Church of Scotland, as part of the Holy Catholic or Universal Church worshipping one God, Father, Son, and Holy Spirit, affirms anew its belief in the Gospel of the sovereign grace and love of God, wherein through Jesus Christ, His only Son, our Lord, incarnate, crucified, and risen, He freely offers to all men, upon repentance and faith, the forgiveness of sins, renewal by the Holy Spirit, and eternal life, and calls them to labour in the fellowship of faith for the advancement of the kingdom of God throughout the world.

The Church of Scotland acknowledges the Word of God, which is contained in the Scriptures of the Old and New Testaments, to be the supreme rule of faith and life.

The Church of Scotland holds as its subordinate standard the Westminster Confession of Faith, recognizing liberty of opinion on such points of doctrine as do not enter into the substance of the Faith, and claiming the right, in dependence on the promised guidance of the Holy Spirit, to formulate,

* *Where there is no induction to a pastoral charge, the words following are omitted.*

interpret, or modify its subordinate standards: always in agreement with the Word of God and the fundamental doctrines of the Christian Faith contained in the said Confession, of which agreement the Church itself shall be sole judge.

Then the Moderator, addressing the Ordinand, who shall stand and make answer to the questions put to him. shall say:

N. N., in view of this Declaration, you are now required to answer these questions:

DO you believe in one God, Father, Son, and Holy Spirit; and do you confess anew the Lord Jesus Christ as your Saviour and Lord?

Answer. I do.

DO you believe the Word of God, which is contained in the Scriptures of the Old and New Testaments, to be the supreme rule of faith and life?

Answer. I do.

DO you believe the fundamental doctrines of the Christian faith contained in the Confession of Faith of this Church?

Answer. I do.

DO you acknowledge the Presbyterian government of this Church to be agreeable to the Word of God; and do you promise to be subject in the Lord to this Presbytery and to the superior courts of the Church, and to take your due part in the administration of its affairs?

Answer. I do.

DO you promise to seek the unity and peace of this Church; to uphold the doctrine, worship, government, and discipline thereof; and to cherish a spirit of brotherhood towards all the followers of the Lord?

Answer. I do.

ARE not zeal for the glory of God, love to the Lord Jesus Christ, and a desire for the salvation of men, so far as you know your own heart, your great motives and chief inducements to enter into the office of the holy Ministry?

Answer. They are.

DO you engage in the strength of the Lord Jesus Christ to live a godly and circumspect life; and faithfully, diligently, and cheerfully to discharge the duties of your ministry, seeking in all things the advancement of the kingdom of God?

Answer. I do.

*DO you accept and close with the call to be Pastor of this Charge, and promise through grace to study to approve yourself a faithful Minister of the Gospel among this people?

Answer. I do.

After the questions have been answered to the satisfaction of the Presbytery, the Moderator shall call upon the Ordinand to sign the Formula, saying:

YOU are required now to sign the appointed Formula as a seal of these vows which you have made.

Then shall be sung the hymn, Veni Creator Spiritus, Come, Holy Ghost, our souls inspire.

* *Where there is no induction to a pastoral charge, this question is omitted.*

Thereafter, the Ordinand shall kneel, and the Moderator, by prayer with laying on of hands, in which all the Ministers present shall join, shall ordain him to the Office of the holy Ministry, saying:

Moderator. Lift up your hearts;

Answer. We lift them up unto the Lord.

Moderator. Let us give thanks unto our Lord God;

Answer. It is meet and right so to do.

IT is verily meet, right, and our bounden duty, that we should at all times and in all places give thanks unto Thee, O Holy Lord, Father Almighty, Everlasting God; who, of Thine infinite love and goodness towards us, hast given to us Thine only Son Jesus Christ to be our Redeemer and the Author of everlasting life, and hast exalted Him unto Thy right hand, whence, according to Thy will, He hath sent down the Holy Spirit and given gifts unto men. We thankfully acknowledge Thy great mercy in bestowing upon us these inestimable benefits; and, we humbly beseech Thee, SEND DOWN THY HOLY SPIRIT UPON THIS THY SERVANT, WHOM WE, IN THY NAME, AND IN OBEDIENCE TO THY MOST BLESSED WILL, DO NOW, BY THE LAYING ON OF OUR HANDS,

Here the Moderator shall lay his hands upon the head of the Ordinand, the other Ministers also laying on their right hands.

ORDAIN AND APPOINT TO THE OFFICE OF THE HOLY MINISTRY IN THY HOLY CATHOLIC CHURCH, COMMITTING UNTO HIM AUTHORITY TO MINISTER THY

WORD AND SACRAMENTS, AND TO BEAR RULE IN THY FLOCK. Impart to him such fullness of Thy grace as shall fit him more and more for the work to which he has been called. Give him counsel, understanding, and utterance, that he may boldly proclaim Thy Word and will. Make him a light unto them that sit in darkness, a watchful and loving guardian over Thy fold, and a follower of the Good Shepherd who gave His life for His sheep. Enable him to guide aright the people of his charge, and in all things to fulfil his ministry without reproach in Thy sight; so that he may abide steadfast to the end, and be received with all Thy faithful servants into Thine eternal joy; through Jesus Christ our Lord, who liveth and reigneth, and is worshipped and glorified, with Thee, O Father, and the Holy Spirit, one God, world without end. AMEN.

AND now, as our Saviour Christ hath taught us, we pray, saying:

OUR Father ...

The Prayer being ended, the newly ordained Minister shall stand, and the Moderator shall say to the people:

Let all present stand.

Then, addressing the newly ordained Minister, he shall say:

I NOW declare you ordained to the Office of the holy Ministry.*

* *Where there is no induction to a pastoral charge, the words following, down to* induct you to this charge, *and the address of the Moderator to the people with their assent (i.e. the portions here enclosed in* [ ]) *shall be omitted.*

C

[AND in the Name of the Lord Jesus Christ, the King and Head of the Church, and by authority of this Presbytery, I induct you to this charge;] and in token thereof we give you the right hand of fellowship.

THE grace of the Lord Jesus Christ be with you.

Then the Moderator, and the other Presbyters in succession, shall give him the right hand of fellowship.

[*When all are seated, the Moderator, addressing the people, shall say:*

BRETHREN of the congregation, Forasmuch as this sacred act involves solemn obligations on your part, I put to you the appointed question:

DO you, the members and adherents of this congregation, receive N. N., whom you have called to be your Minister, promising him all due honour and support in the Lord; and will you give of your means, as the Lord shall prosper you, for the maintenance of the Christian Ministry and the furtherance of the Gospel?

Will you signify your assent by rising and standing in your places?

This having been done, he shall say:

Let all be seated.]

Then shall be sung the hymn, Pour out Thy Spirit from on high.

Thereafter the Moderator shall give to the newly

ordained Minister, who shall stand to receive it, the Charge following:

BELOVED brother: Forasmuch as thou, N. N., art called by Almighty God of His fatherly love, to the ministry of the Word and Sacraments and art this day ordained thereunto by the Church [and appointed to the Pastoral Charge of M.], I now charge thee in the name of the Church to walk worthy of the vocation wherewith thou art called, with all lowliness and meekness, with longsuffering, forbearance, and peaceful endeavour, for the perfecting of the saints, for the work of the ministry, for the upbuilding of the Body of Christ.

Take heed unto thyself and unto all the flock over which the Holy Spirit doth make thee overseer. Love Christ and feed His flock, taking the oversight thereof, not as though thou wert lord over the people committed to thee, but being an example to all in word, in conduct, in charity, in spirit, in faith, and in purity. Give attendance to reading, to exhortation, and to teaching. Neglect not the gift that is in thee, which was given thee with the laying on of the hands of the presbytery. Endure hardness as a good soldier of Jesus Christ. Pray always, watching thereunto with all perseverance. Thus shalt thou save both thyself and those that hear thee; and in that day when the chief Shepherd shall appear thou shalt receive a crown of glory which fadeth not away.

Now the God of peace, that brought again from the dead our Lord Jesus, that great Shepherd of the sheep, through the blood of the everlasting covenant, make you perfect in every good work to do His will, working in you that which is wellpleasing in

His sight, through Jesus Christ; to whom be glory for ever and ever. Amen.*

Then the Moderator shall give to the congregation, who shall stand to receive it, the Charge following:

AND now, beloved brethren of this congregation, you have heard the solemn vows which N. N. has taken, and the obligations laid upon him as your Minister in the Lord. I therefore charge you to reverence and uphold him, in virtue of his office and authority as a Minister of Christ, set over you to lead and guide you in the true way of life.

Forsake not the assembling of yourselves together. Be hearers and doers for the Word which the Lord's servant shall speak in His Name. Avail yourselves of the Sacraments which he has been ordained to minister. Seek the blessing and counsel of the Lord at his hands, and uphold him with your love and fellowship. Grudge not your offerings for the provision of the Lord's house and the work of His kingdom. Continually remember your Minister in your prayers, entreating for him, and for yourselves, the outpouring of the Holy Spirit, that you may be able to know and do the will of God. These things observe to do, so that, at the appearing of the Lord Jesus, you all, pastor and people, may be presented, holy and unspotted, by Him before the face of the Father, in the unity of the one Body, with exceeding joy.

And unto the same our Lord Jesus Christ, with the Father and the Holy Spirit, be ascribed in the

---

* *Where the newly ordained Minister is not inducted to a parochial charge, the service shall end here with a closing hymn or psalm and the Benediction.*

Church all honour and glory, might, majesty, dominion, and blessing, now, henceforth, and for-ever. AMEN.

Then the Moderator shall say:

Let us pray.

ALMIGHTY God, who, under Thine ever-blessed Son, the great Shepherd of the sheep, hast appointed them to be fed and guided by Thy ministering servants; we thank Thee that Thou hast this day provided a pastor for this people; and we earnestly beseech Thee to make Thy servant suffi-cient for the work to which he has been called. Bless the ministry now begun to the spiritual nourishment and growth in grace of this people. Grant that they may be enlightened and edified by the preaching of the Word, quickened by Thy Spirit, sustained by Thy sacraments, established in all holy living, and kept by Thy power through faith unto salvation; through Jesus Christ our Lord, to whom, with Thee and the Holy Spirit, be all honour and glory, world without end. AMEN.

Then shall be sung Psalm cxxii. 6–9, *to the tune* St. Paul, *concluding with the doxology; and the Moderator shall pronounce the Benediction:*

THE peace of God, which passeth all understand-ing, keep your hearts and minds in the know-ledge and love of God, and of His Son Jesus Christ our Lord; and the blessing of God Almighty, the Father, the Son, and the Holy Ghost, be amongst you, and remain with you, always. AMEN.

3

AT THE ORDINATION OF
A MISSIONARY

*When the Ordinand is to be a Foreign Missionary, the
Service of Ordination shall be used as on the pages
preceding to the beginning of page 14. Then the Moderator shall ask the Ordinand the questions appointed,
with the exception of the last; and after the Formula
has been signed, the Ordinand shall kneel, and the
Moderator, by prayer with laying on of hands in
which all the Ministers present shall join, shall ordain him to the Office of the holy Ministry, saying:*

LIFT up your hearts;
  Answer. We lift them up unto the Lord.
Moderator. Let us give thanks unto our Lord God;
Answer. It is meet and right so to do.

IT is verily meet, right, and our bounden duty, that
we should at all times and in all places give thanks
unto Thee, O Holy Lord, Father Almighty, Everlasting God; who, of Thine infinite love and goodness
towards us, hast given to us Thine only Son Jesus
Christ to be our Redeemer and the Author of everything
lasting life, and hast exalted Him unto Thy right
hand, whence, according to Thy will, He hath sent
down the Holy Spirit and given gifts unto men.
We bless Thy Name that Thou hast given the word
of the Cross to lighten them that sit in darkness and

in the shadow of death, and to guide sinful men into the way of peace.

And we give Thee thanks for Thy faithful servants who have gone as Thine ambassadors to peoples that have not known Thy Name. Graciously accept this Thy servant now before Thee, as he dedicates to this high service his life and all its powers; and, we humbly beseech Thee, SEND DOWN THY HOLY SPIRIT UPON HIM AS, IN THY NAME, AND IN OBEDIENCE TO THY MOST BLESSED WILL, WE DO NOW, BY THE LAYING ON OF OUR HANDS,

(*Here the Moderator shall lay his hands upon the head of the Ordinand, the other Ministers also laying on their right hands.*)

ORDAIN AND APPOINT HIM TO THE OFFICE OF THE HOLY MINISTRY, AND SET HIM APART TO THE MISSIONARY SERVICE OF THY HOLY CATHOLIC CHURCH, COMMITTING UNTO HIM AUTHORITY TO MINISTER THY WORD AND SACRAMENTS, AND TO BEAR RULE IN THY FLOCK. Keep him mindful of the greatness of his task and of his unworthiness as Thy servant, that his sufficiency may be in Thee alone. Be with him in all his wayfaring, over land and water; and bestow on him health and strength. Arm him against temptation, and endue him with Thy Spirit, that in zeal and perseverance he may never fail. In loneliness and weariness sustain him by Thy presence, and supply all his need according to Thy riches in glory by Christ Jesus.

Give him deep and understanding sympathy with the people among whom he is to labour. Make him ready to learn as well as teach, to receive as well as give; and grant him by life and doctrine to bring Thy light into dark lives and guide them to the knowledge of Thy Son. Enable him always so to fulfil his calling that, when his service on earth is accomplished, he may be counted with those who, having turned many to righteousness, shine as the stars for ever and ever; through Jesus Christ our Lord, who liveth and reigneth, and is worshipped and glorified, with Thee, O Father, and the Holy Ghost, one God, world without end. AMEN.

AND now, as our Saviour Christ hath taught us, we pray, saying:

OUR Father . . .

Then the Moderator shall say to the people,

Let all present stand.

And, addressing the newly ordained Minister, he shall say,

I NOW declare you ordained to the Office of the holy Ministry, and set apart as a Missionary of the Cross; in token whereof we give you the right hand of fellowship.

THE grace of the Lord Jesus Christ be with you.

Then shall be sung the hymn, Pour out Thy Spirit from on high, *or* O Spirit of the living God.

Thereafter the Moderator shall give to the newly ordained Minister, who shall stand to receive it, the Charge following:

BELOVED brother: Forasmuch as thou, N. N., art called by Almighty God of His fatherly love, to the ministry of the Word and Sacraments and art this day ordained thereunto by the Church, I now charge thee in the name of the Church to walk worthy of the vocation wherewith thou art called, with all lowliness and meekness, with longsuffering, forbearance, and peaceful endeavour, for the perfecting of the saints, for the work of the ministry, for the upbuilding of the Body of Christ.

Take heed unto thyself and unto all the flock over which the Holy Spirit shall make thee overseer. Love Christ and feed His flock, taking the oversight thereof, not as though thou wert lord over the people committed to thee, but being an example to all in word, in conduct, in charity, in spirit, in faith, and in purity. Give attendance to reading, to exhortation, and to teaching. Neglect not the gift that is in thee, which was given thee with the laying on of the hands of the presbytery. Endure hardness as a good soldier of Jesus Christ. Pray always, watching thereunto with all perseverance. Thus shalt thou save both thyself and those that hear thee; and in that day when the chief Shepherd shall appear thou shalt receive a crown of glory which fadeth not away.

Now the God of peace, that brought again from the dead our Lord Jesus, that great Shepherd of the sheep, through the blood of the everlasting covenant, make you perfect in every good work to do His will, working in you that which is wellpleasing in His sight, through Jesus Christ; to whom be glory for ever and ever. Amen.

Then shall be sung Psalm cxxii. 6–9, *to the tune* St. Paul, *concluding with the doxology; and the Moderator shall pronounce the Benediction.*

4

FORM AND ORDER FOR THE INDUCTION OF A MINISTER ALREADY ORDAINED

The Presbytery having been constituted by the Moderator, the Edict shall be produced, duly executed; the prescribed intimation shall be made concerning objections, and, if none be offered, the Presbytery shall resolve to proceed with the Induction.

Divine Service shall begin with the singing of Psalm xlv. *1–4, to the tune* St. Stephen, *concluding with the doxology.*

After which, the Service shall proceed as on pp. 9–12, up to and including the Sermon.

Thereafter, the Narrative shall be read, and, the Minister to be inducted having taken his place before the Presbytery, the Moderator shall say:

IN the Name of the Lord Jesus Christ, the King and Head of the Church, who, being ascended on high, hath given gifts unto men for the edifying of the body of Christ, we are met here as a Presbytery to induct N. N. into the Pastoral Charge of M.

In this act the Church of Scotland, as part of the Holy Catholic or Universal Church worshipping one God, Father, Son, and Holy Spirit, affirms anew its belief in the Gospel of the sovereign grace and love of God, wherein through Jesus Christ, His only Son, our Lord, incarnate, crucified, and risen, He freely offers to all men, upon repentance and faith, the forgiveness of sins, renewal by the Holy Spirit, and eternal life, and calls them to labour in the fellowship of faith for the advancement of the kingdom of God throughout the world.

The Church of Scotland acknowledges the Word of God which is contained in the Scriptures of the Old and New Testaments to be the supreme rule of faith and life.

The Church of Scotland holds as its subordinate standard the Westminster Confession of Faith, recognizing liberty of opinion on such points of doctrine as do not enter into the substance of the Faith, and claiming the right, in dependence on the promised guidance of the Holy Spirit, to formulate, interpret, or modify its subordinate standards: always in agreement with the Word of God and the fundamental doctrines of the Christian Faith contained in the said Confession, of which agreement the Church itself shall be sole judge.

Then the Moderator, addressing the Minister to be inducted, who shall stand and make answer to the questions put to him, shall say:

N. N., in view of this Declaration, you are now required to answer these questions:

DO you believe in one God, Father, Son, and Holy Spirit; and do you confess anew the Lord Jesus Christ as your Saviour and Lord?

Answer. I do.

DO you believe the Word of God, which is contained in the Scriptures of the Old and New Testaments, to be the supreme rule of faith and life?

Answer. I do.

DO you believe the fundamental doctrines of the Christian faith contained in the Confession of Faith of this Church?

Answer. I do.

DO you acknowledge the Presbyterian government of this Church to be agreeable to the Word of God; and do you promise to be subject in the Lord to this Presbytery and to the superior courts of the Church, and to take your due part in the administration of its affairs?

Answer. I do.

DO you promise to seek the unity and peace of this Church; to uphold the doctrine, worship, government, and discipline thereof; and to cherish a spirit of brotherhood towards all the followers of the Lord?

Answer. I do.

ARE not zeal for the glory of God, love to the Lord Jesus Christ, and a desire for the salvation of men, so far as you know your own heart, your great motives and chief inducements to enter into the office of the holy Ministry?

Answer. They are.

DO you engage in the strength of the Lord Jesus Christ to live a godly and circumspect life; and faithfully, diligently, and cheerfully to discharge the duties of your ministry, seeking in all things the advancement of the kingdom of God?

Answer. I do.

DO you accept and close with the call to be Pastor of this Charge, and promise through grace to study to approve yourself a faithful Minister of the Gospel among this people?

Answer. I do.

ERRATA

Page 26, line 9, Psalm xlv *should read* lxv.

Page 28, lines 22 ff. This question should read:
'ARE not zeal for the glory of God, love to the Lord Jesus Christ, and a desire for the salvation of men, so far as you know your own heart, your great motives and chief inducements to enter into this Ministry?'

Ordinal and Service Book of the Church of Scotland

this Thy servant, to fit him more and more for the work to which he has been called. Give him utterance that he may boldly make known Thy Word and will, and faithfully minister Thy sacraments.

Endue him with wisdom and zeal to rule aright the people over whom he is set, and to preserve them in peace and purity; so that this parish, under his administration and example, may increase in grace and holiness. Grant him meekness, patience, and firmness to bear all the trials and troubles of his ministry; and strengthen him with Thy Spirit, that he may abide steadfast to the end, and be received, with all Thy faithful servants, into the joy of his Lord; through the same Jesus Christ our Lord. AMEN.

O GOD, who didst vouchsafe to enlighten the minds of the disciples by the outpouring of the Spirit of Life and Truth; visit, we beseech Thee, this people with Thy love and favour, and bless the ministry now begun to their spiritual nourishment and growth in grace. Grant that they may be enlightened and edified by the preaching of the Word, quickened by Thy Spirit, sustained by Thy sacraments, established in all holy living, and kept by Thy power through faith unto salvation; through Jesus Christ our Lord, who liveth and reigneth with Thee and the Holy Spirit, one God, world without end. AMEN.

OUR Father . . .

The Prayer being ended, the newly inducted Minister shall rise from his knees, and the Moderator shall say to the people:

Let all present stand.

Then, addressing the Minister to be inducted, he shall say:

IN the Name of the Lord Jesus Christ, the King and Head of the Church, and by authority of this

Presbytery, I induct you to this Charge; and in token thereof we give you the right hand of fellowship.

THE grace of the Lord Jesus Christ be with you.

Then the Moderator, and the other Presbyters in succession, shall give him the right hand of fellowship.

When all are seated, the Moderator, addressing the people, shall say:

BRETHREN of the congregation, Forasmuch as this solemn act involves obligations on your part, I put to you the appointed question:

DO you, the members and adherents of this congregation, receive N. N., whom you have called to be your Minister, promising him all due honour and support in the Lord, and will you give of your means, as the Lord shall prosper you, for the maintenance of the Christian Ministry and the furtherance of the Gospel?

Will you signify your assent by rising and standing in your places?

This having been done, he shall say:

Let all be seated.

Then shall be sung the hymn, Pour out Thy Spirit from on high.

Thereafter, the Moderator shall give to the newly inducted Minister, who shall stand to receive it, the Charge following:

BELOVED brother: Forasmuch, as thou, N. N., called by Almighty God, of His fatherly love, to the ministry of the Word and Sacraments, and ordained aforetime thereunto by the Church, art now appointed to the Pastoral Charge of M., I charge thee anew in the name of the Church to walk worthy of the vocation wherewith thou art called, with all lowliness and meekness, with longsuffering, forbearance, and peaceful endeavour, for the perfecting of the saints, for the work of the ministry, for the upbuilding of the Body of Christ.

Take heed unto thyself and unto all the flock over which the Holy Spirit doth make thee overseer. Love Christ and feed His flock, taking the oversight thereof, not as though thou wert lord over the people committed to thee, but being an example to all in word, in conduct, in charity, in spirit, in faith, and in purity. Give attendance to reading, to exhortation, and to teaching. Neglect not the gift that is in thee, which was given thee with the laying on of the hands of the presbytery. Endure hardness as a good soldier of Jesus Christ. Pray always, watching thereunto with all perseverance. Thus shalt thou save both thyself and those that hear thee; and in that day when the chief Shepherd shall appear thou shalt receive a crown of glory which fadeth not away.

Now the God of peace, that brought again from the dead our Lord Jesus, that great Shepherd of the sheep, through the blood of the everlasting covenant, make you perfect in every good work to do His will, working in you that which is wellpleasing in His sight, through Jesus Christ; to whom be glory for ever and ever. Amen.

Then the Moderator shall give to the congregation, who shall stand to receive it, the Charge following:

AND now, beloved brethren of this congregation, you have heard the solemn vows which N. N. has taken, and the obligations laid upon him as your Minister in the Lord. I therefore charge you to reverence and uphold him, in virtue of his office and authority as a Minister of Christ, set over you to lead and guide you in the true way of life.

Forsake not the assembling of yourselves together. Be hearers and doers of the word which the Lord's servant shall speak in His Name. Avail yourselves of the Sacraments which he has been ordained to minister. Seek the blessing and counsel of the Lord at his hands, and uphold him with your love and fellowship. Grudge not your offerings for the provision of the Lord's house and the work of His kingdom. Continually remember your Minister in your prayers, entreating for him, and for yourselves, the outpouring of the Holy Spirit, that you may be able to know and do the will of God. These things observe to do, so that, at the appearing of the Lord Jesus, you all, pastor and people, may be presented, holy and unspotted, by Him before the face of the Father, in the unity of the one Body, with exceeding joy.

And unto the same our Lord Jesus Christ, with the Father and the Holy Spirit, be ascribed in the Church all honour and glory, might, majesty, dominion, and blessing, now, henceforth, and forever. AMEN.

Then shall be sung Psalm cxxii. 6–9, *to the tune* St. Paul, *concluding with the doxology; and the Moderator shall pronounce the Benediction:*

THE peace of God, which passeth all understanding, keep your hearts and minds in the knowledge and love of God, and of His Son Jesus Christ our Lord; and the blessing of God Almighty, the Father, the Son, and the Holy Ghost, be amongst you, and remain with you always. AMEN.

5

AT THE INDUCTION OF
A PROFESSOR

When a Professor is to be inducted to a Chair in a College or University, the Service of Induction shall be used as in the pages preceding to the end of p. 27.

Then the questions appointed shall be asked by the Moderator, except the last question; and thereafter the Formula shall be signed.

Then shall be sung the hymn Veni Creator Spiritus, Come, Holy Ghost, our souls inspire.

After which the Professor to be inducted shall kneel, and the Moderator shall offer this prayer following, saying,

Let us pray.

ALMIGHTY and everlasting God, who hast created us for Thyself so that we can find rest only in Thee; we bless Thee that in eternal love Thou hast taken upon Thee to deliver man. We praise Thy holy Name for the gift of Jesus Christ Thy Son to be our Saviour and Lord, for His redeeming Passion, and His rising again to power over sin and death. We praise Thee for Thy Church, the Body of Christ, and its witness of Thy great salvation; and we give Thee thanks for all true ministers of the Word and doctors of sacred truth from age to age; through the same Jesus Christ our Lord. AMEN.

WE give thanks, O God, for Thy servant now before Thee, and for his gifts and learning; and, as we have charged him with this office, we beseech Thee to send down upon him the Spirit of power, love, and wisdom, that his heart and mind may be stayed on Thee. In Thy Name may he teach those who are to teach others, confirming their faith, enriching their knowledge, and fitting them more and more to serve Thy people in the Gospel. Enable him to fulfil his ministry without blame or reproach, to abide therein steadfastly unto the end, and at the last to enter into Thine eternal kingdom; through Jesus Christ our Lord. AMEN.

POUR out Thy benediction, we beseech Thee, on this College and University. Grant to those who study here such purity of heart and strength of purpose, that no selfish passion may hinder them from knowing Thy will, no weakness from doing it; but in Thy light may they see light clearly, and in Thy service find perfect freedom; through Jesus Christ our Lord, whom with Thee, O Father, and the Holy Spirit, we worship and glorify, world without end. AMEN.

OUR Father . . .

Then the Moderator shall say to the people,

　　Let all present stand.

And addressing the newly inducted Professor, he shall say,

I NOW declare you inducted into the Chair of (*Here the chair shall be named*) in this University (*or* College).

I CHARGE thee in the name of the Church to walk worthy of the vocation wherewith thou art called, with all lowliness and meekness, with long-suffering, forbearance, and peaceful endeavour, for the perfecting of the saints, for the work of the ministry, for the upbuilding of the Body of Christ.

Take heed unto thyself, and unto those over whom the Holy Spirit doth set thee as teacher. Love Christ, and feed those committed to thee, not as though thou wert lord over them, but being an example to all in word, in conduct, in charity, in spirit, in faith, and in purity. Give attendance to reading, to exhortation, and to teaching. Neglect not the gift that is in thee, which was given thee with the laying on of the hands of the presbytery. Endure hardness as a good soldier of Jesus Christ. Pray always, watching thereunto with all perseverance. Thus shalt thou save both thyself and those that hear thee; and in that day when the chief Shepherd shall appear thou shalt receive a crown of glory which fadeth not away.

Now the God of peace, that brought again from the dead our Lord Jesus, that great Shepherd of the sheep, through the blood of the everlasting covenant, make you perfect in every good work to do His will, working in you that which is wellpleasing in His sight, through Jesus Christ; to whom be glory for ever and ever. Amen.

Then shall be sung Psalm cxxii. 6–9, *to the tune* St. Paul, *concluding with the doxology; and the Moderator shall pronounce the Benediction.*

6

FORM AND ORDER FOR THE CELEBRATION OF THE LORD'S SUPPER OR HOLY COMMUNION IN COURTS OF THE CHURCH

Psalm xliii. 3–5 *shall be sung to the tune* Martyrs, Caithness, *or* Invocation.

After which, all standing, the Moderator shall say:

WHAT shall we render unto the Lord for all His benefits toward us? We will take the cup of salvation, and call upon the Name of the Lord. We will pay our vows unto the Lord now in the presence of all His people.

Let us pray.

ALMIGHTY God, unto whom all hearts be open, all desires known, and from whom no secrets are hid; cleanse the thoughts of our hearts by the in-spiration of Thy Holy Spirit, that we may perfectly love Thee, and worthily magnify Thy holy Name: through Christ our Lord. AMEN.

ETERNAL God, our heavenly Father, who ad-mittest Thy people into such wonderful com-munion that, partaking by a divine mystery of the body and blood of Thy dear Son, they should dwell in Him, and He in them; we unworthy sinners, approaching Thy presence and beholding Thy glory, do repent us of our transgressions. We have sinned, we have grievously sinned against Thee, in thought, word, and deed. We have broken our past vows, dishonoured Thy holy Name, and profaned Thy sanctuary. Wherefore we beseech Thee to have mercy upon us.

Most merciful Father, have mercy upon us; for the sake of Jesus Christ, forgive us all our sins; deliver us, by Thy Holy Spirit, from all uncleanness in spirit and in flesh; and enable us heartily to forgive others, as we beseech Thee to forgive us, and to serve Thee henceforth in newness of life, to the glory of Thy holy Name; through Jesus Christ our Lord. AMEN.

O GOD, who hast prepared for them that love Thee such good things as pass man's understanding; pour into our hearts such love toward Thee, that we, loving Thee above all things, may obtain Thy promises, which exceed all that we can desire; through Jesus Christ our Lord, to whom, with Thee and the Holy Spirit, be all honour and glory, world without end. AMEN.

Psalm cxvi. 13–19 *may here be sung to the tune* Kilmarnock, *or to* Jackson.

Then shall be read Lessons from Holy Scripture, of which one shall be from a Gospel, such as Isaiah liii. 1–6; Ephesians iii. 14–21; *and* St. John vi. 47–51.

The Nicene Creed shall next be said by all, standing.

I BELIEVE in one God the Father Almighty, Maker of heaven and earth, And of all things visible and invisible:

And in one Lord Jesus Christ, the only-begotten Son of God, Begotten of His Father before all worlds, God of God, Light of Light, Very God of Very God, Begotten, not made, Being of one substance with the Father, By whom all things were made: Who for us men, and for our salvation, came down from heaven, And was incarnate by the Holy Ghost of the Virgin Mary, And was made man, And was crucified also for us under Pontius Pilate. He suffered and was buried, And the third day He rose again according to the Scriptures, And ascended into heaven, And sitteth on the right hand of the Father. And He shall come again with glory to judge both the quick and the dead: Whose kingdom shall have no end.

And I believe in the Holy Ghost, The Lord, and Giver of Life, Who proceedeth from the Father and the Son, Who with the Father and the Son together is worshipped and glorified, Who spake by the prophets. And I believe one Holy Catholic and Apostolic Church. I acknowledge one Baptism for the remission of sins. And I look for the Resurrection of the dead, And the Life of the world to come. AMEN.

Then shall the Moderator say,

Let us pray.

O GOD, our heavenly Father, we beseech Thee to hear the intercessions which we offer through the mediation of Thy well-beloved Son.

REMEMBER, O Lord, Thy holy Church throughout the world, and reveal Thy glory among all nations. Save Thy people, and bless Thine inheritance; feed them also, and lift them up for ever.

REMEMBER, O Lord, us Thy servants assembled now before Thee as a court and council of Thy Church, and shed down upon us Thy heavenly wisdom and grace.

REMEMBER, O Lord, our kindred and friends; and encompass them with Thy loving kindness and tender mercy.

REMEMBER, O Lord, the sick and the suffering, the aged and the dying, and all who are in loneliness, sorrow, or bereavement; and those whom we name in silence before Thee. Visit them with Thy love and consolation, and grant them Thy peace; through Jesus Christ our Lord. AMEN.

AND rejoicing in the communion of saints, we remember with thanksgiving before Thee, O Lord, Thy saints of every age and place, all Thy faithful servants, and those dear to us, who are at rest in Thee. Keep us in unbroken fellowship with thy whole Church in heaven and on earth, and grant us at last to rejoice together in Thine eternal kingdom; through Jesus Christ our Lord, who liveth and reigneth, and is worshipped and glorified, with Thee, O Father, and the Holy Spirit, world without end. AMEN.

Here, if desired, a devotional address may be given.

After which shall be sung Psalm xxiv. 7–10, *to the tune* St. Magnus *or* St. George's Edinburgh; *or the hymn,* Ye servants of the Lord *or* And now, O Father, mindful of the love.

During the singing, the Elders shall bring in the Elements, and place them on the Holy Table.

Thereafter, the Moderator shall unveil the Elements, and, the singing being ended, shall say:

Let us pray.

O GOD, who by the blood of Thy dear Son hast consecrated for us a new and living way into the holiest of all; grant us, we beseech Thee, the assurance of Thy mercy, and sanctify us by Thy heavenly grace; so that, with a pure heart and a cleansed conscience, we may offer unto Thee a sacrifice in righteousness, and duly celebrate this holy Sacrament to the glory of Thy Name; through Jesus Christ our Lord. AMEN.

Then the Moderator shall say:

THE grace of the Lord Jesus Christ be with you all.

BELOVED in the Lord, Attend to the words of the institution of the Holy Supper of our Lord Jesus Christ, as they are delivered by the Apostle Paul.

I have received of the Lord that which also I delivered unto you, That the Lord Jesus the same night in which He was betrayed took bread: and when He had given thanks, He brake it, and said, Take, eat: this is My body, which is broken for you: this do in remembrance of Me. After the same manner also He took the cup, when He had supped, saying, This cup is the new testament in My blood: this do ye, as oft as ye drink it, in remembrance of Me. For as often as ye eat this bread, and drink this cup, ye do show the Lord's death till He come.

THEREFORE, that we may fulfil His institution in righteousness and joy, let us follow His blessed example in word and action: IN THE NAME OF THE FATHER, AND OF THE SON, AND OF THE HOLY GHOST.

AS the Lord Jesus, the same night in which He was betrayed, took bread, I take these elements of bread and wine to be set apart from all common uses to this holy use and mystery; and as He gave thanks and blessed, let us draw nigh to God, and present unto Him our thanksgivings and prayers.

> THE Lord be with you;
> *And with Thy spirit.*
> Lift up your hearts;
> *We lift them up unto the Lord.*
> Let us give thanks unto our Lord God;
> *It is meet and right so to do.*

IT is verily meet, right, and our bounden duty, that we should at all times, and in all places, give thanks unto Thee, O Holy Lord, Father Almighty, Everlasting God; who didst create the heavens and the earth and all that is therein; who didst make man in Thine own image, and whose tender mercies are over all Thy works.*

THEE, mighty God, heavenly King, we magnify and praise. With angels and archangels and with all the company of heaven, we worship and adore

* *Here may be added the Proper Preface according to the season of the Christian Year, as in the Book of Common Order.*

Thy glorious name; evermore praising Thee and saying:

HOLY, Holy, Holy, Lord God of Hosts,
Heaven and earth are full of Thy glory:
Glory be to Thee, O Lord Most High.

BLESSED is he that cometh in the name of
the Lord:
Hosanna in the highest.

VERILY holy, verily blessed, art Thou, Almighty
and Merciful God, who didst so love the world
that Thou gavest Thine only-begotten Son, that
whosoever believeth in Him should not perish but
have everlasting life.

Not as we ought, but as we are able, do we bless
Thee for his holy incarnation, for His perfect life
on earth, for His precious sufferings and death upon
the Cross, for His glorious resurrection and ascen-
sion, for His continual intercession and rule at Thy
right hand, for the promise of His coming again, and
for His gift of the Holy Spirit.

WHEREFORE, having in remembrance the
work and passion of our Saviour Christ, and
pleading His eternal sacrifice, we Thy servants do
set forth this memorial, which He hath commanded
us to make; and we most humbly beseech Thee to
send down Thy Holy Spirit to sanctify both us and
these Thine own gifts of bread and wine which we
set before Thee, that the bread which we break may
be the Communion of the body of Christ, and the
cup of blessing which we bless the Communion of
the blood of Christ; that we, receiving them, may by
faith be made partakers of His body and blood, with

all His benefits, to our spiritual nourishment and growth in grace, and to the glory of Thy most holy Name.

AND here we offer and present unto Thee ourselves, our souls and bodies, to be a reasonable, holy, and living sacrifice; and we beseech Thee mercifully to accept our sacrifice of praise and thanksgiving, as in fellowship with all the faithful in heaven and on earth, we pray Thee to fulfil in us, and in all men, the purpose of Thy redeeming love; through Jesus Christ our Lord, by whom, and with whom, in the unity of the Holy Spirit, all honour and glory be unto Thee, O Father Almighty, world without end. AMEN.

AND now, as our Saviour Christ hath taught us, we humbly pray, saying:

OUR Father . . .

Then the Moderator shall say:

ACCORDING to the holy institution, example, and command of our Lord Jesus Christ, and for a memorial of Him, we do this: who, the same night in which He was betrayed, TOOK BREAD

(*here the Moderator shall take the bread into his hands*),

and when He had blessed, and given thanks, HE BRAKE IT

(*here he shall break the bread*),

and said,

TAKE, EAT: THIS IS MY BODY, WHICH IS BROKEN FOR YOU: THIS DO IN REMEMBRANCE OF ME.

After the same manner also, HE TOOK THE CUP

(here he shall raise the cup),

saying:

THIS CUP IS THE NEW COVENANT IN MY BLOOD: THIS
DO YE, AS OFT AS YE DRINK IT, IN REMEMBRANCE OF
ME.

LAMB of God, that takest away the sins of the
world, have mercy upon us.
Lamb of God, that takest away the sins of the world,
have mercy upon us.
Lamb of God, that takest away the sins of the world,
grant us Thy peace.

*Then the Moderator shall himself partake in both
kinds; afterwards serving those Ministers and Elders
who are assisting him; and, in giving the bread, he
shall say:*

TAKE ye, eat ye; this is the body of Christ which
is broken for you: this do in remembrance of
Him.

And, in giving the cup:

THIS cup is the new covenant in the blood of
Christ, which is shed for many unto remission
of sins: drink ye all of it.

*When all have received, and the bread and wine have
been replaced on the Holy Table and covered, the
Moderator shall say:*

THE PEACE OF THE LORD JESUS CHRIST BE WITH YOU
ALL.

Then shall he call the People to thanksgiving, saying:

Let us pray.

ALMIGHTY and ever-living God, we most
heartily thank Thee that in Thy great love Thou
dost vouchsafe to feed us at Thy Table with this
spiritual food, and dost thereby assure us of Thy
favour and goodness towards us; and that we are
very members incorporate in the mystical body of
Thy Son, the blessed company of all faithful people,
and are also heirs through hope of Thy everlasting
kingdom. And we most humbly beseech Thee, O
heavenly Father, so to assist us with Thy grace, that
we may continue in this holy fellowship, and live
henceforth to Thy glory; through Jesus Christ our
Lord. AMEN.

AND rejoicing in the communion of saints, we
thank and praise Thee for all Thy servants who
have departed in the faith; the great cloud of witnesses by which we are compassed about; all Thy
saints in every age who have loved Thee in life and
continued faithful unto death; especially those dear
to our own hearts. Give us grace to follow them
as they followed Christ; and bring us with them, at
the last, to those things which eye hath not seen, nor
ear heard, which Thou hast prepared for them that
love Thee; through Jesus Christ our Lord, who
liveth and reigneth, and is worshipped and glorified,
with Thee, O Father, and the Holy Spirit, world
without end. AMEN.

Then shall be sung Psalm ciii. 1–5, Paraphrase lx, *or
other psalm or hymn of praise.*

Thereafter, the Moderator shall pronounce the Benediction:

THE peace of God, which passeth all understanding, keep your hearts and minds in the knowledge and love of God, and of His Son Jesus Christ our Lord; and the blessing of God Almighty, the Father, the Son, and the Holy Ghost, be amongst you, and remain with you always. AMEN.

The Elements shall then be reverently removed from the church, while all stand, during which Nunc Dimittis, *or* Paraphrase xxxviii. 8, 10, 11 *may be sung.*

7

FORM AND ORDER
FOR THE
BURIAL OF A MINISTER

I. In Church

The coffin having been borne into the church and placed within the Sanctuary in front of the Holy Table,* the Service shall begin with the singing of a psalm or portion of a psalm, such as Psalm ciii. 13–18, *to the tune* Kilmarnock, *and thereafter the Minister shall say one or more of these Sentences following:*

OUR help is in the Name of the Lord, who made heaven and earth.

LIKE as a father pitieth his children, so the Lord pitieth them that fear Him. For He knoweth our frame; He remembereth that we are dust.

CAST Thy burden upon the Lord, and He shall sustain thee. In His favour is life: weeping may endure for a night, but joy cometh in the morning.

THEY that be wise shall shine as the brightness of the firmament; and they that turn many to righteousness as the stars for ever and ever.

* *The coffin shall be decently covered with a pall, and the robes of the deceased Minister placed thereon. The coffin shall be at right angles to the Holy Table, with the head towards the congregation.*

REMEMBER them that had the rule over you, which spake unto you the Word of God; and considering the issue of their life, imitate their faith.

BLESSED be God, even the Father of our Lord Jesus Christ, the Father of mercies, and the God of all comfort; who comforteth us in all our tribulation, that we may be able to comfort them which are in any trouble, by the comfort wherewith we ourselves are comforted of God.

Let us pray.

ETERNAL God, our heavenly Father, who lovest us with an everlasting love, and canst turn the shadow of death into the morning; help us now to wait upon Thee with reverent and submissive hearts. In the silence of this hour speak to us of eternal things, that through patience and comfort of the Scriptures we may have hope, and be lifted above our darkness and distress into the light and peace of Thy presence; through Jesus Christ our Lord. AMEN.

ALMIGHTY God, who art our refuge and strength, and a very present help in time of trouble; enable us, we pray Thee, to put our trust in Thee; and seeing that we have an High Priest who is touched with the feeling of our infirmities, may we come boldly unto the throne of grace, that we may obtain mercy, and find grace to help in time of need; through the same Jesus Christ our Lord, who liveth and reigneth with Thee and the Holy Spirit, one God, for evermore. AMEN.

Then shall be said or sung one or more of the following or other suitable psalms; Psalm xxiii, xxxiv, xc, ciii. 8–18, cxxi, cxxx, *concluding with the doxology.*

Thereafter shall be read passages from the New Testa-
ment, one or more of these following: Rom. viii. 35–
39, 1 Cor. xv. 20–23, 35–38, 42–44, 50–58, 2 Cor.
v. 1–10, 1 Pet. i. 3–9, Rev. vii. 13–17, Rev. xxi. 1–7.
After which shall be read this passage from the Gos-
pel: St. John xiv. 1–6, 27.

At the end of the reading from Holy Scripture, the
reader shall say:

T HE Lord bless to us the reading of His holy
Word, and to His name be glory and praise.
AMEN.

Then shall be sung a portion of a psalm, such as Psalm
lxxiii. 23–26, *to the tune* St. Mary; *or a hymn, such*
as O Lord of life where'er they be *or* For those we
love within the veil, *to the tune* Es ist kein Tag.

Then shall the Minister say:

L IFT up your hearts;
Answer. We lift them up unto the Lord.

Minister. Let us give thanks unto our Lord God;

Answer. It is meet and right so to do.

And the Minister shall continue as follows:

I T is verily meet, right, and our bounden duty,
that we should at all times and in all places give
thanks unto Thee, O Holy Lord, Father Almighty,
Everlasting God, who didst make man in Thine own
image, and when he had fallen from Thee didst
redeem him, and didst bring life and immortality
to light in the gift of Thy Son, our Saviour Jesus
Christ. Most humbly and heartily we give Thee
thanks, that by His death He destroyed the power of
death, and by His glorious resurrection opened the

kingdom of heaven to all believers. Grant us assuredly to know that because He lives we shall live also, and that neither death nor life, nor things present nor things to come, shall be able to separate us from Thy love, which is in Christ Jesus our Lord, who liveth and reigneth with Thee and the Holy Spirit, one God, for evermore. AMEN.

FATHER of mercies, and God of all comfort, look in Thy tender love and pity, we beseech Thee, on Thy sorrowing servants. Enable them to find in Thee their refuge and strength, a very present help in trouble, and to know the love of Christ, which passeth knowledge. Grant them faith and hope in Him who by death hath conquered death, and by rising again hath opened the gates of everlasting life; even Jesus Christ our Lord. AMEN.

ETERNAL Father, who holdest all souls in life; we give Thee humble thanks for Thy goodness unto this our brother departed. For what Thou enabledst him to do and to be that was wellpleasing in Thy sight; for his faith in Thy holy Name; for his devotion to the service of Thy house; for his faithful ministry in Thy Church and within this parish; for his courage, charity, and constancy, we give Thee thanks and praise. We thank Thee that for him all sickness and sorrow are ended, that death itself is past, and we pray that he may enter into the rest that remaineth for Thy people; through Jesus Christ our Lord. AMEN.

AND we beseech Thee, Almighty God, that we, being inspired by the example of Thy saints, may run with patience the race that is set before us, looking unto Jesus, the author and finisher of our faith; so that, when this mortal life is ended, we may be gathered with those whom we have loved in the kingdom of Thy glory, where there shall be no more death, neither sorrow nor crying, neither shall there be any more pain, for the former things are passed away; through Jesus Christ our Lord, who liveth and reigneth, and is worshipped and glorified, with Thee, O Father, and the Holy Ghost, one God, world without end. AMEN.

AND now, as our Saviour Christ hath taught us, we humbly pray, saying:

OUR Father . . .

Then shall be sung Paraphrase xlii *to the tune* Dunfermline, *or* Paraphrase lxi *to the tune* Effingham, *or other suitable hymn; and thereafter, the Benediction shall be pronounced:*

THE peace of God, which passeth all understanding, keep your hearts and minds in the knowledge and love of God, and of His Son Jesus Christ our Lord; and the blessing of God Almighty, the Father, the Son, and the Holy Ghost, be amongst you, and remain with you always. AMEN.

While the coffin is being removed from the church there may be sung the hymn, Nunc Dimittis, Lord, now lettest Thou thy servant depart in peace, *or* Paraphrase xxxviii. 8–11 *to the tune* St. Andrew.

II. AT THE GRAVE

The coffin having been placed in the grave, the Minister, standing at the foot, shall say:

I AM the Resurrection and the Life, saith the Lord; he that believeth in Me, though he were dead, yet shall he live; and whosoever liveth and believeth in Me shall never die.

FORASMUCH as it hath pleased Almighty God to take unto Himself the soul of our brother here departed, we therefore commit his body to the ground; earth to earth, ashes to ashes, dust to dust; in sure and certain hope of the resurrection to eternal life through Jesus Christ our Lord, who shall fashion anew this body of our humiliation that it may be like unto the body of His glory, according to the mighty working whereby He is able to subdue all things unto Himself.

I HEARD a voice from heaven saying unto me, Write, Blessed are the dead which die in the Lord from henceforth: Yea, saith the Spirit, that they may rest from their labours; and their works do follow them.

Let us pray.

ALMIGHTY God, who by the death of Thy dear Son hast destroyed death, by His rest in the tomb hast sanctified the graves of Thy saints, and by His glorious resurrection hast brought life and immortality to light; receive, we beseech Thee, our unfeigned thanks for that victory over death and the grave which He hath obtained for us and for all who sleep in Him. Keep us in everlasting fellowship with all that wait for Thee on earth, and with all that stand around Thy throne in heaven: in union with Him who is the Resurrection and the Life, who liveth and reigneth with Thee and the Holy Spirit, ever one God, world without end. AMEN.

ALMIGHTY and most merciful God, who in Thy providence hast hidden from our eyes that which is yet to be, but hast given us in Thy Son Jesus Christ the Light of life in which we may walk and not stumble; enable us to walk in that Light all the rest of our time, whether it be long or short; that amid the shadows and uncertainties, the trials and perils, of this passing world, we may neither fear nor falter, and may come at last beyond all shadow and separation to our perfect fulfilment in Thee, where is no darkness, but light for evermore; through the same Jesus Christ our Lord. AMEN.

NOW the God of peace, that brought again from the dead our Lord Jesus, that great Shepherd of the sheep, through the blood of the everlasting covenant, make you perfect in every good work to do His will, working in you that which is well-pleasing in His sight, through Jesus Christ, to whom be glory for ever and ever. AMEN.

8

PRAYERS FOR CONSTITUTING A MEETING OF A COURT OF THE CHURCH

ALMIGHTY God, our heavenly Father, who art the strength and stay of all who trust in Thee; we humble ourselves before the throne of Thy glory, and praise Thy Name for Thine infinite love to men in Jesus Christ Thy Son. We thank Thee for the Church which He established to be Thy witness to the world, wherein Thou hast called us to be His servants, setting us in office as overseers of Thy flock.

O Lord our God, who didst promise Thy Holy Spirit to the first disciples, that they might minister in their Master's Name to a world in need, impart unto us the same grace, we beseech Thee, that we in our day may be enabled to fulfil our high calling. Inasmuch as Thou dost lay on us a task so great, make Thy grace sufficient for us, and perfect Thou Thy strength in our weakness; for the sake of Jesus Christ our Lord. AMEN.

WITH humble hearts, O righteous Father, we acknowledge our unworthiness before Thee. Have compassion upon our ignorance; pardon our failures and misdeeds; and if, through blindness, wilfulness, or sloth, we have swerved in aught from the path of faith and obedience, recall us in Thy mercy, and let not Thy flock suffer through our fault. So purify our souls, we beseech Thee, by Thine indwelling Spirit, that being filled with Thy love and the zeal of Thy House, we may serve Thee henceforth with undivided heart; through Jesus Christ our Lord. AMEN.

ALMIGHTY God, we pray for Thy whole Church. Pour forth upon her Thy Holy Spirit.

Give grace and power to all missionaries of the Cross; that the ends of the earth may speedily see the salvation of our God.

We pray for our country and commonwealth, for Elizabeth our Queen, and for all in authority over us; that our peoples may be ruled with wisdom and integrity and be taught that righteousness which alone exalteth a nation.

For the homes of the people we beseech Thee, that they may be built upon a sure foundation of love and piety; that fathers may be true priests within the family, and that under them children may grow up in the nurture and admonition of the Lord, to the increase of the Church, the welfare of the State, and the peace of the world.

Hear our prayers for the parishes of our care; that they may be established in their holy Faith, and abound in good works with thanksgiving.

Have pity upon the poor, the distressed in body or in mind, and all who are in sorrow or mourning, especially those whom we name in our hearts before Thee. . . . Be mindful in Thy mercy of those of our own brethren who are restrained by Thy providence from assembling with us this day, and bless them according to their several needs; through Jesus Christ our Lord. AMEN.

AND now as, in Christ's Name, we constitute ourselves a court of Thy Church, we beseech Thee
to endue us with wisdom and grace, and so to direct
our deliberations by Thy Holy Spirit, that in all we
decide and do, Thy will may be done, and Thy kingdom advanced; through Jesus Christ our Lord, who
liveth and reigneth with Thee and the Holy Spirit,
one God, for evermore. AMEN.

OUR Father . . .

II

ALMIGHTY God, who art the Creator and Lord
of all things, we bless and praise Thy Name that
in Jesus Christ Thy Son we have beheld Thy glory
and Thy love, and have known Thee to be the everlasting Father and Saviour of men. We give thanks
for the infinite blessing Thou hast wrought for men
through Thy Church, for Thy faithfulness to her
throughout all generations, and for the rich inheritance into which we have entered through the faith
and patience of all who have loved and served her
in the past; through Jesus Christ our Lord. AMEN.

O LORD our God, who hast called us to be fellow
labourers with Thee in Thy Church and in the
world; we acknowledge ourselves unworthy, and
confess our manifold sin. Forgive, we beseech Thee,
the weakness of our faith, the coldness of our love,
the poverty of our service. Search us, O Lord, and
know our hearts, try us and know our thoughts; and
see if there be any wicked thing in us, and lead us in
the way everlasting; for the sake of Jesus Christ our
Lord and Saviour. AMEN.

GOD of all truth and grace, without whom we can do nothing; settle and confirm in us our faith in Christ; strengthen us in fidelity to His will; deepen our joy in His service; and in all the duties of our calling enable us effectually to fulfil the work Thou givest us to do, for the good of Thy Church and the glory of Thy Name; through the same Jesus Christ our only Lord and Redeemer. AMEN.

GRACIOUS Father, we humbly beseech Thee for Thy Church throughout all the world. Send down Thy heavenly grace upon those whom Thou hast called to serve Thee in the Gospel at home and abroad, that they may be holy and obedient, and fulfil with diligence their several ministries. Hasten the time when Thy children everywhere shall be brought to new life and liberty by the preaching of the Gospel, and bind the nations closer in the bonds of common service and interest; that they may be delivered from the scourge of war, and learn the things that belong unto their peace; through Jesus Christ our Lord. AMEN.

REMEMBER, O Lord, our country and its dominions and dependencies. Give Thy grace to Elizabeth our Queen, and to all who bear office throughout the realm, that in all things we may be governed righteously and in Thy fear; and grant unto us, not only such outward prosperity as may seem good to Thee, but above all things, such virtue and true religion that Thy holy Name may be glorified among us; through Jesus Christ our Lord. AMEN.

FATHER most merciful, we commend to Thy goodness those who suffer in body, mind, or estate; those who are in peril, or have been bereaved; that they may be cherished by Thy compassions, upheld by Thy grace, and comforted by Thy love; through Jesus Christ our Lord. AMEN.

AND now, O Lord God, by whose Spirit the whole Church is governed and sanctified; we beseech Thy blessing as we constitute ourselves a court of Thy Church in the Name of our only King and Head. Grant us the illumination of Thy Holy Spirit, that we may have a right judgement in all things, and that in the work Thou givest us to do we may truly and godly serve Thee, to the glory of Thy Name and the good of Thy Church; through Jesus Christ our Lord, who liveth and reigneth with Thee and the Holy Spirit, one God, world without end. AMEN.

OUR Father . . .

III

ALMIGHTY God, who art glorious in holiness, full of love and compassion, abundant in grace and truth; all Thy works praise Thee in all places of Thy dominion, and Thy Son hath glorified Thee on earth. Praise waiteth for Thee in Zion, and unto Thee shall the vow be performed.

Most pitiful and loving Father, whose love can never fail us; pardon in us, we humbly beseech Thee, all that is wayward and rebellious, all that is thankless and forgetful. Restore unto us the light of Thy presence and the comfort of Thy Spirit; granting us, with the forgiveness of our sins, true repentance of the same, and grace and power to forsake them forthwith; through Jesus Christ our Lord. AMEN.

O LORD our God, who art the only Founder and Keeper of Thy Church; we thank Thee that Thou hast received us into the communion of Thy well-beloved Son, and called us to share with Him the work of winning men for Thy kingdom. Forasmuch as we have not chosen Thee, but Thou hast chosen us, we pray for grace to give ourselves wholly to this our task and service. Thou who art all-holy, grant us sincerity and singleness of mind. Hold ever before us the example of our Master, who pleased not Himself, but gave Himself up for us all, that, sharing His ministry and consecration, we may enter into His joy and His reward; through the same Jesus Christ our Saviour. AMEN.

O GOD of unchangeable power and eternal light; look favourably upon Thy whole Church, and especially upon this the Church of our fathers, that Thy people everywhere may serve and glorify Thee in all holiness of life, and Thy kingdom be strengthened and advanced; through Jesus Christ our Lord. AMEN.

O GOD, the Father of all mankind, we pray for the nations of the earth, and for kings, princes, and rulers; especially for Thy servant Elizabeth our Queen, for her whole Council, and for the people of this realm; and grant that all things may be so ordered and settled that truth and justice, piety and peace, may be established among us to all generations; through our Lord and Saviour Jesus Christ. AMEN.

M ERCIFUL Lord, we commend unto Thee the people of our care, and beseech Thee to bless their labours for Thy Church. Let the prayers of those who cry out of tribulation come unto Thee; that they may rejoice to find that Thy mercy is present to their need. Graciously heal the sick, give rest to the weary, have compassion upon the suffering, comfort the afflicted, and save the dying; through Jesus Christ our Lord. AMEN.

O GOD, who hast promised to those who trust in Thee the grace of Thy Holy Spirit; as now we constitute ourselves a court of Thy Church in the Name of Jesus Christ our Lord, we beseech Thee to give us by the same Spirit good understanding of all that we ought to do, and bless our deliberations and endeavours for the welfare of Thy Church and the advancement of Thy kingdom; through Jesus Christ our Lord, who liveth and reigneth with Thee and the Holy Spirit, world without end. AMEN.

OUR Father . . .

IV

ALMIGHTY God, most holy and most high, look graciously on us Thy servants who bow humbly before Thee, and grant us Thy blessing as we are met together in the Name of Jesus Christ Thy Son. Now, as at all times, we magnify and praise Thee for Thine inestimable love to the world revealed in Him, our Saviour. We praise Thee for the Church He founded to carry forward the work of His Gospel, and thank Thee that Thou hast called us, though unworthy, to a holy service in the same. Pardon us those things wherein we have been unprofitable servants in the past; make us more worthy of our high vocation; cause us to abound ever more and more in the fruits of the Spirit; and so enrich us with Thy heavenly grace that we may be faithful, wise, and loving in the fulfilment of our office, and may adorn the doctrine of God our Saviour with righteous and godly lives; through Jesus Christ our Lord. AMEN.

O GOD, the Father of all mankind, we beseech Thee to hear us for those whom we ought to remember when we intercede at Thy throne of grace.

Bless abundantly Thy holy Catholic Church in all her branches and ministries. Especially we pray Thee to continue Thy favour, which has been from of old, to the Church of our fathers. Throughly furnish her for Thy service in the Gospel: give her strength for her great tasks; keep her faithful amid all change to the trust committed to her charge; and prosper all the work Thou hast given her to do at home and abroad.

Hear us as we commend to Thee those who have gone forth at Thy call into distant lands, to proclaim the word of life to those who know it not. Cheer and sustain them with the constant assurance of Thy presence, and enable them so to lift up Christ in the glory of His love and power to save, that all men may be drawn unto Him; to whom be dominion for evermore. AMEN.

GOD of our fathers, who in days past hast been favourable to our land; hear our prayer for our country and for the British Commonwealth of nations. God save the Queen, and bless her and the Royal Family in their labours for the welfare of the people. So direct by thy counsel the Queen's Ministers and advisers that they may in all things be servants of Thy holy will. Give guidance, we beseech

Thee, to the High Court of Parliament, and to all in places of authority and power throughout the land, especially . . . (*here mention may be made of the Lord Provost, the Provost, Magistrates, Council, and public officials of the city, town, or county in which the Presbytery is met*). Enlighten them with wisdom, and keep them mindful of the trust committed to them; through Jesus Christ our Lord. AMEN.

MOST gracious God, who art the strength of the weak and the refuge of the sorrowful; we bear on our hearts before Thee the sick, the sad, and the sorrowing, and all who anywise suffer in body, mind, or worldly estate, especially our brethren who are absent by reason of sickness or infirmity. Draw near to the sick with sustaining strength and healing; speak to the downcast and desolate in comfort and peace; and to those who are appointed to die, grant the safe keeping of Thy love and in due time a peaceful entrance into rest; through Jesus Christ our Lord. AMEN.

ETERNAL God, with whom are the issues of life; we give Thee thanks for all Thy faithful servants who, having witnessed in their lives a good confession, have left the light of their example to shine before Thy people. Mercifully grant that by the power of Thy Spirit we may be enabled to follow them in all godly living and faithful service, and that hereafter we may with them behold Thy face in glory and serve Thee in Thy heavenly kingdom; through Jesus Christ our Lord. AMEN.

AND now, most merciful Father, whose we are and whom we serve, as we constitute ourselves a court of Thy Church in the Name of Jesus Christ, our King and Head, we beseech Thee to vouchsafe to us the guidance of Thy good Spirit, that all we devise and do may be for the welfare of Thy Church, for the progress of Thy kingdom, and for the glory of Thy great and holy Name; through Jesus Christ our Lord, who liveth and reigneth with Thee and the Holy Spirit, one God, for evermore. AMEN.

OUR Father . . .

9

PRAYERS FOR CONSTITUTING A SPECIAL MEETING OF A COURT OF THE CHURCH

I

PREVENT us, O Lord, in all our doings with Thy most gracious favour, and further us with Thy continual help; that in all our works begun, continued, and ended in Thee, we may glorify Thy holy Name, and finally by Thy mercy obtain everlasting life; through Jesus Christ our Lord. AMEN.

OUR Father . . .

II

O GOD, forasmuch as without Thee we are not able to please Thee; mercifully grant that Thy Holy Spirit may in all things direct and rule our hearts; through Jesus Christ our Lord. AMEN.

OUR Father . . .

III

ALMIGHTY God, who hast founded Thy Church upon earth, and hast promised to abide with it for ever; look upon us in Thy mercy, and vouchsafe unto us Thy guidance and blessing, as we are here assembled as a court thereof; and bestow upon us the wisdom that is from above, which is first pure, then peaceable, gentle, and easy to be entreated, full of mercy and good fruits; through Jesus Christ our Lord. AMEN.

OUR Father . . .

IV

O GOD, who hast taught us in all our ways to acknowledge Thee, and hast promised that Thou wilt direct our paths; aid and direct us, we beseech Thee, in our deliberations as a court of Thy Church; that all that we think and do may be in accordance with Thy will, for the blessing of Thy people and for the glory of Thy holy Name; through Jesus Christ our Lord. AMEN.

OUR Father . . .

V

G LORY be to the Father, and to the Son, and to the Holy Spirit;
As it was in the beginning, is now, and
ever shall be, world without end. AMEN.

A LMIGHTY God, we humble ourselves in Thy holy presence, confessing our weakness and unworthiness, and asking for Thy help and grace. Unable of ourselves to do what is right, we beseech Thee to undertake for us according to Thine infinite mercies; in Jesus Christ our Lord. AMEN.

O GOD of our salvation, we pray for the Holy Catholic Church, that Thou wouldst protect and prosper it, and fill all Thy people with Thy Spirit, that they may be drawn ever closer to Thee and nearer to one another.

We pray for Thy Church in this land, that

ministers and members may labour together as loyal fellow servants in the unity of the Spirit. Revive Thy work and bless Thine inheritance; through Jesus Christ our Lord. AMEN.

O LORD our God, whose wisdom is infinite and whose power is almighty; we humbly beseech Thee to guide us by Thy Holy Spirit, as we constitute ourselves a court of Thy Church, that in all we are called to consider we may be enabled clearly to know Thy will and faithfully to do it; through Jesus Christ our Lord. AMEN.

OUR Father . . .

VI

At a Meeting for the Translation of a Minister
(Following one of the above)

REGARD with Thy gracious favour, O Lord, Thy servant whom we are about to translate; and, as he goes forth from amongst us, let Thine abundant blessing go with him, and strengthen him for all his future labours. Endue him richly with Thy Holy Spirit, and give him grace and guidance for all the duties to which Thou hast called him; that he may abound in zeal for Thy Church and diligence in Thy service, and at last receive the crown of glory that passeth not away; through Jesus Christ our Lord. AMEN.

VII

At a Meeting for sustaining a Call to a Minister
(Following one of the above)

LET Thy rich blessing, we beseech Thee, O Lord, rest upon Thy servant, about to be called to the charge of a parish and congregation in our midst. Vouchsafe unto him a full measure of Thy Spirit, and endue him with gifts of faith and love, of wisdom and knowledge, and of devotion to his Lord and Master. Grant that he may be a faithful shepherd of the sheep, feeding them with the Bread of Life, watching over them with prayerfulness, and tender care, and leading them in the paths of holiness and peace. And for those over whom he is to be appointed we pray, that they may wait with open hearts upon Thy word, and receive with joyfulness the mysteries of Thy Gospel; that both he and they may grow together in the knowledge of Thy will and in the service of Thy kingdom; through Jesus Christ our Lord. AMEN.

10

PRAYERS FOR THE INDUCTION OF A MODERATOR OF A COURT OF THE CHURCH

I

ALMIGHTY God, who, for the work of Thy Son's kingdom, hast sanctified in all ages the men of Thy right hand to be Ministers in Thy Church, and, through His Apostles, didst order the governance thereof; mercifully behold Thy servant N., whom we have elected to be Moderator in this court of Thy Church. Bestow upon him, we beseech Thee, the spirit of wisdom and understanding, of counsel and strength, that he may fulfil his office to the glory of Thy Name and the welfare of Thy flock; for the sake of the Good Shepherd who giveth His life for the sheep, even Jesus Christ, Thy Son, our Lord. AMEN.

II

ALMIGHTY God, our heavenly Father, who in Thine infinite love toward men hast founded Thy Church on earth, and hast appointed us, Thine unworthy servants, to the office of the ministry therein; uphold by the power of Thy Holy Spirit our brother N., whom we have called to the chief place among us at this time. Endue him with strength of body and soundness of mind; and grant him such faith, wisdom, and grace as shall enable him to fulfil his duties for the edifying of Thy Church; through Jesus Christ Thy Son, its King and Head, to whom be glory for ever. AMEN.

11

FORM AND ORDER OF DIVINE SERVICE FOR THE UNION OF CONGREGATIONS

The Congregations being assembled, the Minister shall say:

LET us worship God.

Then shall be sung Psalm cii. 13–18 (second version) *to the tune* Duke Street.

The psalm being ended, and while the people continue standing, the Minister shall say:

OUR help is in the Name of the Lord, who made heaven and earth.

THIS is the day which the Lord hath made: we will rejoice and be glad in it.

THE Lord hath done great things for us, whereof we are glad.

O GIVE thanks unto the Lord; for He is good; for His mercy endureth for ever.

Let us pray.

ALMIGHTY and everlasting God, the Father of our Lord and Saviour Jesus Christ, who art infinite in power and glory, and boundless in love; we Thy servants come into Thy House in the multitude of Thy mercy, rejoicing in the great things

Thou hast done for us, and adoring Thee for Thy loving kindness and Thy truth; and we beseech Thee to regard us with Thy favour, to inspire us by Thy Holy Spirit, and to accept the prayers which we offer unto Thee; in the Name of Jesus Christ our Lord. AMEN.

O GOD most holy and most merciful, we humbly confess in Thy presence that we have sinned against Thee, and are unworthy of the least of all Thy mercies. We have wandered from Thy paths; we have been unfaithful to the trust committed unto us; we have failed in faith, hope, and charity. By our blindness and waywardness, by our lack of brotherly love, and by our distrust of Thy promises, we have grieved Thy Holy Spirit, and have come far short of Thy glory.

Most merciful Father, grant unto us, we humbly beseech Thee, pardon and remission of all our sins; bestow on us the grace of a true repentance; and enable us to return unto Thee with all our hearts; through Jesus Christ our Lord. AMEN.

ALMIGHTY God, who hast exalted Thy Son Jesus Christ to be Head over all things to the Church, and hast willed that all should be one in Him; we give Thee humble and hearty thanks for Thy great goodness toward us.

For the Church which Thou hast established to be Thy witness before men, for Thy love and faithfulness to it from generation to generation, for the grace which Thou gavest unto our fathers, and for the heritage of faith and toil and sacrifice into which we have entered, we praise and bless Thy Name.

For Thy forbearance with us in our errors and

divisions, and for the mercy with which Thou hast forgiven and overruled them, we praise and bless Thy Name.

For the building again of the broken walls of Thy Church in our land, and for the call Thou hast given to us to seek the unity that becometh brethren in Christ Jesus, we praise and bless Thy Name.

For the grace with which Thou hast guided our counsels, removing hindrances out of the way, and bringing us together in peace and concord as brethren united in the Lord, we with one heart and mind do adore Thee and praise Thy glorious Name.

And now, O Lord, we beseech Thee so to endue us with singleness of mind and purity of heart, that no selfish passion may hinder us from knowing Thy will, and no weakness from doing it; that in Thy light we may see light, and in Thy service find perfect freedom. Unite our hearts in faith and hope, lead us continually by Thy Spirit; and grant that, being rooted and grounded in love, we may be able to comprehend with all saints what is the breadth and length and depth and height, and to know the love of Christ which passeth knowledge, that we may be filled with all the fullness of God; to whom, Father, Son, and Holy Spirit, be all honour and praise, world without end. AMEN.

Then shall be read a Lesson from the Old Testament, Isaiah lxi.

The hymn, Thy hand, O God, has guided, *may now be sung, or,* The Church's one foundation, *or* Christ is made the sure foundation.

Then shall be read Lessons from the New Testament, Ephesians iv. 1–16 *and* St. John xvii. 19–23.

Then shall all, standing, make common confession of their faith, saying,

I BELIEVE in God the Father Almighty, Maker of Heaven and earth:

And in Jesus Christ His only Son our Lord, Who was conceived by the Holy Ghost, Born of the Virgin Mary, Suffered under Pontius Pilate, Was crucified, dead, and buried, He descended into hell; The third day He rose again from the dead, He ascended into heaven, And sitteth on the right hand of God the Father Almighty; From thence He shall come to judge the quick and the dead.

I believe in the Holy Ghost; The Holy Catholic Church; The Communion of Saints; the Forgiveness of sins; The Resurrection of the body; And the life everlasting. AMEN.

Then shall the Minister say,

Let us pray.

A LMIGHTY God, eternal Father, who hast promised to reveal Thy glory in Christ Jesus among all nations; we beseech Thee in His Name to hear our humble intercessions.

O God, who lovest Thy people with an everlasting love, and hast purchased them unto Thyself with the blood of Thy dear Son; we pray for the whole congregation of the faithful, that Thou wouldst draw them nearer to Thee and to each other in the bonds of a holy faith, and cause them to abound in truth and love, in unity and peace, and in devotion to their Lord and Saviour.

We pray especially for Thy Church in this land, that, as Thou hast knit Thy people together in a closer fellowship, so Thou wouldst endue them more richly with Thy heavenly grace. Revive Thy work, O Lord; increase Thy kingdom of righteousness and peace; and hasten the time when in the Name of Jesus every knee shall bow, and every tongue confess that He is Lord.

Lord God of our fathers, who from age to age hast led Thy people in Thy ways; we pray for our country with all its dominions and dependencies, that Thou wouldst exalt it in righteousness, and keep us faithful to the trust which Thou hast committed to our charge. Regard with Thy favour our sovereign lady Elizabeth, our Queen, and all the Royal House. Bless all in authority throughout the commonwealth. And grant unto all nations that they may be bound together in brotherhood and guided in the ways of peace, to the glory of Thy holy Name.

O God of all compassion, we pray for the poor, the sick, the suffering, and the sad, and for those whom we name in our hearts before Thee; that Thou wouldst sustain them by Thy presence, and comfort them with Thy love; through Jesus Christ our Lord. AMEN.

Thereafter shall be sung the paraphrase, O God of Bethel.

Then shall a Sermon be preached, concluding with an Ascription of Praise; after which the Offerings may be received.

The hymn, Veni Creator Spiritus, Come, Holy Ghost, our souls inspire *shall now be sung, or other suitable hymn.*

Thereafter, the Minister shall say:

DEARLY beloved brethren; Whereas the Congregation of N. Church, and the Congregation of N. Church in this place, have resolved to unite and form one Congregation, on the basis of union adopted on . . .; and whereas the Presbytery of M. did on . . . direct that the union so agreed upon should be effected today; now therefore I call upon you, who as members of these congregations are about to enter into this solemn covenant, to attend to the vow in which you are asked to pledge yourselves.

IN THE NAME OF THE FATHER, AND OF THE SON, AND OF THE HOLY GHOST. AMEN.

DO you, members of the Congregations of N. Church and of N. Church, having agreed to come together and to be one Congregation in Christ Jesus, under the designation of N. Church, pledge yourselves, in the presence of God Most High, to be faithful to the covenant of unity, love, and peace into which you are entering, for the better service of Christ's kingdom and the glory of His Name?

Will you signify your assent by rising and standing in your places?

When the people have risen, and are still standing, the Minister shall say:

TO the glory of God the Father, who has called us by His grace:

And of His Son Jesus Christ, who loved us and gave Himself for us:

And of the Holy Spirit, who illumines and sanctifies us:

We consecrate this union.

IN the unity of the faith:
In the communion of saints:

In love and goodwill toward all:

In gratitude for the labours and the sacrifice of our fathers:

In loving remembrance of those who have finished their course:

Acknowledging that without us their work is not made perfect:

We dedicate ourselves to the worship of God and the service of His kingdom.

IN THE NAME OF THE FATHER, AND OF THE SON, AND OF THE HOLY GHOST. AMEN.

NOW, therefore, in the Name of the Lord Jesus Christ, the only King and Head of His Church, I declare you to be united in one congregation.

BEHOLD, how good and how pleasant it is for brethren to dwell together in unity.

THE Lord bless you, and keep you: the Lord make His face shine upon you, and be gracious unto you: the Lord lift up His countenance upon you, and give you peace. AMEN.

Let us pray.

O LORD our God, Almighty and Everlasting, who by Thy good hand upon us hast brought us unto this hour in unity of spirit and in the bond of peace; we bless Thee that Thou hast sent down Thy

Holy Spirit upon us, knitting us together in one communion and fellowship through Jesus Christ Thy Son.

And now, in His Name, as we have constituted ourselves one Congregation of Thy people, we pray Thee, without whom nothing can prosper, to confirm and bless our act; that we may join ourselves in a perpetual covenant that shall not be broken.

And we beseech Thee, gracious Father, to receive us as we dedicate ourselves anew to Thy service. Let the fire of Thy love consume in us all self-seeking and self-will; and so sanctify our union by Thy Holy Spirit, that it may be for Thy glory. Bind us closer to one another in worship and work, and enable us with one mind to strive together for the faith of the Gospel. And grant that, as there is one Body, and one Spirit, one Lord, one Faith, one Baptism, one God and Father of all, so we may henceforth be all of one heart and one soul, united in the bond of truth and love, and with one mind and one mouth glorify Thee; through Jesus Christ our Lord. AMEN.

ETERNAL God, with whom do live the spirits of just men made perfect, we bless and praise Thy Holy Name for all Thy servants who have fought a good fight, and finished their course, and kept the faith. We bless Thee for all who have served Thee and their brethren in godliness and truth, and who have handed on to us a goodly heritage. We bless Thee for all who have laboured for the peace and unity of Thy Church, and by faith have seen this day. Wherefore, seeing we are encompassed about with so great a cloud of witnesses, enable us to lay aside every weight, and the sin that doth so easily beset us, and to run with patience the race that is set before us, looking unto Jesus, the author and finisher of our faith. And grant at last that we may be presented with them before the presence of Thy glory with exceeding joy; through the same Jesus Christ our Lord, who liveth and reigneth, and is worshipped and glorified, with Thee, O Father, and the Holy Spirit, world without end. AMEN.

OUR Father . . .

Thereafter, the hymn, Te Deum Laudamus, We praise Thee, O God, *or the hymn,* Now thank we all our God, *shall be sung.*

After which, the Benediction shall be pronounced:

THE peace of God, which passeth all understanding, keep your hearts and minds in the knowledge and love of God, and of His Son Jesus Christ our Lord; and the blessing of God Almighty, the Father, the Son, and the Holy Ghost, be amongst you and remain with you always. AMEN.

12

ORDER OF SERVICE
FOR THE DEDICATION
OF A HALL-CHURCH

The congregation being assembled, the doors shall be closed two minutes before the hour at which the Service is to begin. The presiding Minister shall ask entrance to the church by knocking thrice on the main door, and using these words of Holy Scripture:

OPEN to me the gates of righteousness: I will go into them, and I will praise the Lord.

The door shall then be opened from within. Greeting to the people shall be given from the inner door of the church in these words:

PEACE be to this house, and to all who worship herein.

Peace be to those that enter, and to those that go out herefrom.

Peace be to those that love it, and that love the name of Jesus Christ our Lord.

After which he shall say, Let us worship God.

Then he shall say,
All people that on earth do dwell.

The officiating Ministers and members of Presbytery shall then enter the church, and proceed in order to the places allotted to them, the Presiding Minister going

*to the Holy Table, during which time shall be sung
the metrical* Psalm c, *to the tune* Old Hundredth,
with doxology.

*Then the people, still standing, shall be called to prayer
in these words of Holy Scripture:*

OUR help is in the name of the Lord, who made
heaven and earth.
Except the Lord build the house, they labour in
vain that build it.
O magnify the Lord with me, and let us exalt His
name together.

Let us pray.

BLESSED art Thou, O Lord God of our Fathers:
and to be praised and exalted above all for ever.
Blessed art Thou in the temple of Thine holy glory;
and to be praised and glorified above all for ever.
Blessed art Thou on the glorious throne of Thy
kingdom; and to be praised and glorified above all
for ever.

Glory be to the Father, and to the Son, and to the
Holy Ghost, as it was in the beginning, is now, and
ever shall be, world without end. AMEN.

MOST holy and merciful Father, we acknowledge and confess in Thy presence the sin-
fulness of our nature, and our shortcomings and
offences against Thee. Thou alone knowest how
often we have sinned, in wandering from Thy ways,
in wasting Thy gifts, in forgetting Thy love. Have
mercy upon us, O Lord, who are ashamed and
sorry for all wherein we have displeased Thee.

Almighty God, who freely pardonest all who repent and turn to Thee; fulfil now in every contrite

heart Thy promise of redeeming grace, absolving us from all our sins, and delivering us from an evil conscience; through the perfect sacrifice of Christ our Lord. AMEN.

ALMIGHTY and eternal God, the sanctifier of all things, whose loving kindness never faileth; graciously vouchsafe Thy presence to us here met to dedicate this sanctuary to Thy most holy worship and this building to Thy service; mercifully illumine and brighten it with Thine own glory, and pour down Thy blessing upon us; through Jesus Christ our Lord, who liveth and reigneth with Thee and the Holy Spirit, one God, for evermore. AMEN.

[Then the Ceremony of the Lighting of the Lamps may take place.

Where the lighting of the church has been given by young people of the Church of Scotland who are members of the League of the Lamp, one of their number shall light the lamps, saying these words:

ON behalf of the League of the Lamp, I light the lamps of this Sanctuary. May they shine to the glory of God, and tell of the illumination of His Holy Spirit.

Thereafter shall be read these words of Holy Scripture:

GOD said, Let there be light: and there was light.

The Lord is my light and my salvation.

In Thy light we shall see light.

Blessed is the people that know the joyful sound; they shall walk, O Lord, in the light of Thy countenance.

Then spake Jesus unto them saying: I am the light of the world, he that followeth Me shall not walk in darkness, but shall have the light of life.]

Then shall be sung metrical Psalm xliii. 3–5, *to the tune* Invocation.

Thereafter shall be read a Lesson from the Old Testament, 1 Kings viii. 22–30.

Then shall be sung Paraphrase xx. 1, 2, 5, *to the tune* Irish.

Thereafter shall be read Lessons from the New Testament, Ephesians ii. 13–22 *and* St. Matthew xxi. 12–16.

Then the people standing shall say together the Apostles' Creed:

I BELIEVE in God the Father Almighty, Maker of heaven and earth;

And in Jesus Christ His only Son our Lord, Who was conceived by the Holy Ghost, Born of the Virgin Mary, Suffered under Pontius Pilate, Was crucified, dead, and buried, He descended into hell; The third day He rose again from the dead, He ascended into Heaven, And sitteth on the right hand of God the Father Almighty; From thence He shall come to judge the quick and the dead.

I believe in the Holy Ghost; The holy Catholic Church; The Communion of Saints; The Forgiveness of sins; The Resurrection of the body; And the Life everlasting. AMEN.

After which shall be sung the hymn, Christ is made the sure foundation.

Thereafter, the Sermon shall be preached, concluding with an Ascription of Praise in these words:

NOW unto Him that is able to do exceeding abundantly above all that we ask or think, according to the power that worketh in us; unto Him be glory in the Church by Christ Jesus, throughout all ages, world without end. AMEN.

Then shall be read the Narrative of Proceedings; after which shall be said these words following:

BELOVED brethren, this House, which has been built for the honour and service of Almighty God, we shall now solemnly dedicate unto the Father, the Son, and the Holy Ghost, one living and true God, to whom be glory and majesty, dominion and power, for ever and ever. AMEN.

THE DEDICATION

Then shall be sung the hymn, Veni Creator Spiritus, Come, Holy Ghost, our souls inspire.

Thereafter, the people still standing, the presiding Minister at the Holy Table shall say the Prayers of Dedication following.

Minister. Lift up your hearts;

Answer. We lift them up unto the Lord.

Minister. Let us give thanks unto our Lord God;

Answer. It is meet and right so to do.

IT is very meet, right, and our bounden duty, that we should give thanks unto Thee, O God, whom the heaven of heavens cannot contain, much less this House that we have builded. Thou hast promised that in all places where Thou dost record Thy name, there Thou wilt meet with Thy people to bless them. Therefore we beseech Thee mercifully to receive this House which we offer unto Thee, and to bless this Sanctuary which we now set apart from all common uses for praise and prayer, the reading and preaching of Thy holy Word, and the celebration of Thy holy Sacraments. Grant that this place may be a habitation of Thy glory, so that all who seek Thy presence here may behold Thine everlasting light, and be satisfied with Thine eternal love; through Jesus Christ our Lord, who liveth and reigneth, and is worshipped and glorified, with Thee, O Father, and the Holy Ghost, one God, world without end. AMEN.

The presiding Minister shall then take his place beside the Baptismal Font, and shall say,

JESUS said, All power is given unto me in heaven and in earth. Go ye, therefore, and teach all nations, baptizing them in the name of the Father, and of the Son, and of the Holy Ghost; and, lo, I am with you alway, even unto the end of the world.

IN the name of the Father, and of the Son, and of the Holy Ghost, I dedicate this Font to the glory of God.

Let us pray.

ALMIGHTY God, who hast called us to be members of Thy household and family; bless and sanctify this Font to the holy use which Jesus Christ, Thy Son, hath ordained; and grant that whosoever shall here be baptized with water may be baptized by Thy Holy Spirit and die unto sin and rise again unto righteousness; and, being received into Thy Holy Catholic Church, may ever remain in the number of Thy faithful children; through the same Jesus Christ our Lord. AMEN.

The presiding Minister shall then take his place beside the Lectern, and shall say,

THY word is a lamp unto my feet, and a light unto my path.

IN the name of the Father, and of the Son, and of the Holy Ghost, I dedicate this Lectern to the glory of God.

Let us pray.

BLESSED God, who has caused all Holy Scriptures to be written for our learning, bless this place whereon they rest; and grant that Thy people may in such wise hear them, read, mark, learn, and inwardly digest them, that by patience and comfort of Thy holy word, they may embrace and ever hold fast the blessed hope of everlasting life which Thou hast given us in our Saviour Jesus Christ. AMEN.

The presiding Minister shall then take his place beside the Pulpit, and shall say,

FOR ever, O Lord, Thy word is settled in heaven. Through Thy precepts I get understanding.

IN the name of the Father, and of the Son, and of the Holy Ghost, I dedicate this Pulpit to the glory of God.

Let us pray.

ALMIGHTY God, who dost enlighten the minds of Thy servants with the knowledge of Thy truth; let Thy blessing rest upon this place from which Thy holy word is henceforth to be delivered; and grant that it may not return unto Thee void, but have free course and be glorified, prospering in the thing whereto Thou dost send it, and turning the hearts of men unto Thee; through Jesus Christ our Lord. AMEN.

The presiding Minister shall then take his place behind the Communion Table, and shall say,

THIS is the Table that is before the Lord. They shall enter into my sanctuary and they shall come near to my Table.

Offer the sacrifices of righteousness, and put your trust in the Lord.

IN the name of the Father, and of the Son, and of the Holy Ghost, I dedicate this Table of Communion to the glory of God.

Let us pray.

ETERNAL God, the Father of our Lord Jesus Christ, of whom every family in heaven and earth is named; mercifully bless, hallow, and sanctify at our hands this Holy Table set apart for celebrating the saving mystery of redemption. Grant that when Thy people come hither with penitence, obedient to our Saviour's word, This do in remembrance of Me, they may render unto Thee the sacrifice of thanksgiving, and, receiving the sacrament of His body and blood, be filled with Thy grace and heavenly benediction, and be made partakers of eternal life. Grant also that the prayers and offerings here presented unto Thee may ever come with acceptance before Thy throne; through Him who stands within the veil, our eternal High Priest and Mediator, even Jesus Christ our Lord. AMEN.

AND now as our Saviour Christ hath taught us, we humbly pray, saying,

OUR Father . . .

Silence shall be kept for a brief space, after which the church shall be declared dedicated to the service of Almighty God in these words:

IN the Name of the Father, and of the Son, and of the Holy Ghost, I do now declare this Sanctuary to be consecrated to the worship of Almighty God; and I declare this house to be offered to the service of God and of His people; to whom, God eternal in Trinity, be glory and majesty, dominion and power, for ever and ever. Amen.

Thereafter, the people still standing, there shall be said these words following, in which all shall join:

AND now, as a congregation within the household of God;
In the unity of the Faith;
In the communion of saints;
In goodwill towards all;
In remembrance of those who have finished their course;
In gratitude for the gift of this Sanctuary to be a habitation of God through His Spirit and of this house to be used in His service:

We dedicate ourselves anew to the worship of God
and the service of His kingdom:
In the Name of the Father, and of the Son, and of
the Holy Ghost. Amen.

Then shall be sung metrical Psalm lxxii. 17–19, *to the
tune* Effingham.

*Thereafter, the Offerings shall be received, and the
Prayers of Thanksgiving and General Intercession
shall be said:*

Let us pray.

O GOD, the Father everlasting, from whom
cometh down every good gift and every perfect
gift, graciously accept the offerings which we present unto Thee and dedicate to Thy service. We give
Thee thanks and praise for Thy manifold goodness,
and that Thou hast brought us in safety and gratitude to this hour. We thank Thee for the revelation
of Thyself in Thy holy Word, and in Christ Jesus the
living Word, the Light and the Life of men. Fill us,
we beseech Thee, with such love to Him, that we
may ever abide in Him and He in us, till our lives
are hid with Christ in Thee; through the same Jesus
Christ our Lord. AMEN.

O GOD, most glorious, most bountiful, accept,
we humbly beseech Thee, our praises and
thanksgivings for Thy holy Catholic Church, the
mother of us all who bear the name of Christ; for the
Faith it hath conveyed in safety to our time, and
the mercies by which it hath enlarged and comforted
the souls of men; for the virtues which it hath
established upon earth, and the holy lives by which
it hath glorified Thee; to whom, O blessed Trinity,

be ascribed all honour, might, majesty, and dominion, now and for ever. AMEN.

ALMIGHTY and everlasting God, hear our intercessions for all men which we offer unto Thee through our only Mediator and Advocate, our great High Priest who maketh perpetual intercession for us, even Jesus Christ our Lord.

Remember in Thy mercy Thy holy Church, and especially in this land and parish.

Remember in Thy mercy the whole family of mankind, that they may come to know Thee, the only true God, and dwell together in concord and unity.

Remember in Thy mercy all who bear rule upon earth. Bestow Thy favour upon Elizabeth our Queen and all her house; vouchsafe Thy wisdom and guidance to her counsellors; and pour out the spirit of godliness and peace upon the people of her Commonwealth.

Remember in Thy mercy those who are in affliction or distress, or any sickness of body or mind; support, heal, and strengthen them.

Remember in Thy mercy our own loved ones, that they may be ever in Thy keeping.

We remember before Thee with thankful hearts the saints and martyrs of every age, the faithful departed, and all dear to us. Grant, O Lord, that we with them may come at last to the joy of Thine eternal kingdom where Thy light shineth for evermore; through Jesus Christ our Lord. AMEN.

ALMIGHTY and everlasting God, who of old didst fill with Thy Spirit in wisdom and understanding the builders of Thy Tabernacle; we give

Thee thanks for Thy servants who design and build Thy sanctuaries now, especially those who have laboured upon this House, and beseech Thee to vouchsafe to them Thy grace and blessing; enlighten, purify, direct, and sanctify them; and prosper all endeavours to do greater honour to Thy holy House, and to render the offering of our prayers and praises more worthy of Thy divine Majesty; through Jesus Christ our Lord, to whom with Thee and the Holy Ghost, be glory, dominion, and praise, world without end. AMEN.

Then shall be sung metrical Psalm cxxii, vv. 6–9, *to the tune* St. Paul, *with doxology.*

The Benediction shall be given in these words:

THE peace of God, which passeth all understanding, keep your hearts and minds in the knowledge and love of God, and of his Son Jesus Christ our Lord; and the blessing of God Almighty, the Father, the Son, and the Holy Ghost, be amongst you, and remain with you always. AMEN.

Silence shall be kept for a brief space; after which, the congregation standing, the officiating Ministers and members of the Presbytery shall retire in procession, during which time shall be sung Paraphrase lxv. 5, 6, 7, 10, 11, Hark how the adoring hosts above, *to the tune* St. Magnus.

Note: *If Holy Communion be not celebrated at the Service of Dedication, a celebration shall follow upon the first Sunday thereafter, completing the dedication by putting the building to its full use.*

PRINTED IN
GREAT BRITAIN
AT THE
UNIVERSITY PRESS
OXFORD
BY
CHARLES BATEY
PRINTER
TO THE
UNIVERSITY